JESUS: GOD'S EMPTINESS, GOD'S FULLNESS

THE CHRISTOLOGY OF ST. PAUL

Jennings B. Reid

Paulist Press ■ New York ■ Mahwah, N.J.

Library of Congress Cataloging-in-Publication Data

Reid, Jennings B., 1913–
     Jesus, God's emptiness, God's fullness: the christology of St. Paul / Jennings B. Reid.
         p.   cm.
     Includes bibliographical references and indexes.
     ISBN 0-8091-3165-X
     1. Jesus Christ—History of doctrines—Early church, ca. 30-600.   2. Paul, the Apostle, Saint—Contributions in Christology.   3. Bible.   N.T.   Epistles of Paul —Theology.   I. Title.
BT198.R41315   1990
232'.09'015—dc20
                                                                              90-36837
                                                                                   CIP

Published by Paulist Press
997 Macarthur Boulevard
Mahwah, New Jersey 07430

Printed and bound in the
United States of America

Contents

Dedication

To
Kitty Lou, Carol and Lynn

Preface

Ever since a college course on *The Life and Writings of Saint Paul*, this great apostle has held a special interest for me. Through the years since, my appreciation has grown for his intellectual genius, his theological insights, and his total dedication to Jesus Christ.

Beyond those college days, it has been my privilege to delve more deeply into his views of the person of Jesus Christ, what may be called his "high Christology." This was especially true during a two-year graduate study period at Princeton Theological Seminary and at New College, University of Edinburgh. The more I researched the background of his Christology, the more I came to appreciate his lofty view of Christ, coming from one who had been the arch-enemy of the faith he now so boldly proclaimed.

It is my sincere hope and prayer that readers of these pages will also be led to a deeper appreciation of who Jesus Christ was, and is, as interpreted by Saint Paul.

A Word of Appreciation

It is a privilege to welcome this profound study of Paul's teaching on Christ. Dr. Jennings Reid brings a lifetime of both scholarship and pastoral ministry to bear on the often puzzling multitude of Paul's reflections about this Jesus the Christ whom the apostle served so passionately. Perhaps it is this very breadth of experience that makes Dr. Reid's presentation so sensitive to the many sides of Paul's thought.

For all too long, the discussion of Paul seemed to be mired in the Reformation polemics that pitted Roman Catholic insistence on salvation as sanctification against Protestant justification by faith alone. Dr. Reid transcends this debate by recognizing the paradox at the heart of Paul's preaching: Jesus is both the fullness of God and the emptiness of God. Does Paul have to have a logical theory that is consistently judicial? Or one that views the entire mystery of Christ only in a full ecclesiology? By probing the rich and suggestive language of the Hebrew scriptures from which Paul drew so much of his own nourishment as a Jew and as a disciple of Jesus, the author is able to show that Paul's language is above all the language of covenantal love, and that Jesus' own self-giving is a product of sharing fully in the love of God for the world.

Dr. Reid argues persuasively that Paul indeed had a very high Christology—he calls it a lofty Christology. Yet Paul's Christ was never docetist or gnostic. The Christ was one with the very human Jesus of Nazareth who lived under the Law in order to break open its treasured language of Word, Wisdom, Spirit and Servant to be realized concretely and fully in himself. The emphasis on paradox is key for Reid because only in the humanity of Jesus can the two extremes of saving love be fully reconciled. The word "reconciliation" is the theme motif for this entire book. "God was in Christ reconciling the world to himself" as 2 Corinthians 5:19 puts it from Paul's point of view. The initiative is

3

God's, the healing is God's, the love is God's, but the beloved recipient of it all is our human race. To express this profound truth of love, Paul borrowed the redemption language of the Exodus journey of liberation, the justification language of the prophetic calls to conversion, and the sacrifice language of the liturgy in worship.

Paul was clearly not a man explaining the causes and effects of his religious convictions, but a mystic who was deeply united with the Christ he proclaimed and deeply in love with a God who could have sent such a Son. This is a very well-reasoned and well-argued book, but in the end it is a moving introduction to a new Paul that many of us may never have met before.

Lawrence Boadt, C.S.P.
Editor

Introduction

No one has so influenced the course of human history as Jesus Christ, and no one has been so responsible for the extension of that influence as the apostle Paul. It was Jesus who gave the world a new religion, though deeply rooted in Jewish heritage. It was the apostle Paul, more than any other person, who took what Jesus had done and interpreted it to the far-flung corners of the known world. Surely it was nothing short of miraculous that within a single generation a new religion should have arisen and spread to all the major centers of the Roman empire.

A miracle is wrought by the power of God at work. If the first miracle was the incarnation itself, broadly inclusive of the birth, life, death, and resurrection of Jesus, the second miracle was that a small group of men and women were able, under the guidance of the Holy Spirit, not only to preserve the gospel tradition against overwhelming odds, but to transmit it within half a century to every major center of the empire. The person chiefly responsible for this amazing feat was the apostle Paul.

Moreover, it is the apostle Paul who gives us the loftiest Christology of the New Testament, with the possible exception of John, the fourth evangelist, and in this regard he and John are in accord. The man Jesus was none other than God's eternal Son, the Logos made flesh, the chosen messiah of Israel, the savior of the world.

We cannot say that Paul arrived at his lofty view of Christ by a single leap of faith. The revelation seems to have come to him as a process, though the Damascus road experience was the turning point. Browning, in portraying the last moments of the apostle John, puts these words upon the lips of the dying saint as those gathered around him hovered over him to catch every last syllable:

> What first were guessed as points
>   I now knew stars,
> And named them in the Gospel I have writ.[1]

So it must have been with Paul; what first he guessed as points he now knew as stars, and named them in the epistles which he wrote.

St. Paul's Christology is epitomized in two contrasting statements about the "fullness of God" dwelling in Christ and Christ's "emptying" himself of divine prerogatives to take the form of a servant and dying on a cross. The two statements are from his prison epistles, respectively as follows:

> For in him all the fullness of God was pleased to dwell (Col 1:19; cf. 2:9).

> Have this mind among yourselves, which you have in Christ Jesus, who, though he was in the form of God, did not count equality with God a thing to be grasped, but emptied himself, taking the form of a servant, being born in the likeness of men. And being found in human form he humbled himself and became obedient unto death, even death on a cross (Phil 2:5–8).

Thus the "fullness of God" in Christ, on the one hand, and his "self-emptying" of divine prerogatives, on the other hand, present us with a kind of antithesis, or paradox. The two concepts, held concurrently and equally, provide us with the key to Paul's insight with regard to Christ's person and his effective work of redemption.

The sequence of thought followed in this discourse is as follows: to set the stage, in chapter 1 we shall consider some biographical information on the apostle Paul through whom this amazing revelation came concerning the person of Christ. In chapters 2 and 3 we shall examine the Greek terms *pleroma* (fullness) and *kenosis* (self-emptying) which constitute the paradox in the person of Christ. In the last three chapters we shall show how the paradox relates to the incarnation, the atonement, and the church.

1

The Man Through Whom the Revelation Came

It has been said that a great institution is but the lengthened shadow of a man or woman. In similar vein, it can be said that the rapid growth of Christianity in the first century was the length-ened shadow of a man, and that man was the apostle Paul. No other person is so responsible for making Christianity a world religion as he.

Paul and Jesus were contemporaries, though they grew up in different parts of the empire, and it is doubtful that their paths ever crossed during the earthly life of Jesus. Nevertheless it is an interesting fact that while Jesus was growing up in Galilee and preparing himself for God's work through him, another young man was growing up in another part of the empire and was un-wittingly being prepared as the one eminently qualified to take the work of Jesus and give it a worldwide dimension.

Tarsus, No Mean City

The very place of his birth seemed an act of providence. When Paul told the Roman tribune that he was a native of Tarsus in Cilicia, "a citizen of no mean city," it was an understatement (Acts 21:39). Tarsus had been a leading city of Cilicia from an-cient times, a center of government and commerce. It was the capital city of the province. In 41 B.C. it was made a "free city" by Mark Antony, exempt from taxes, as a reward for its loyalty in opposition to Cassius. This distinction was later renewed by Au-gustus.

It was a harbor city, the harbor being located just six miles to the south but joined to the city by way of a tributary, the river Cydnus, which flowed through the city. This clear and beautiful stream had its source in the Taurus Mountains some thirty miles to the north. Not only was Tarsus a city of commerce by sea, it was also a crossroads of the great land routes. The great Roman road connecting Syria and other lands east and south with Asia Minor ran through Tarsus. To the north was the land route through the Cilician gates connecting Tarsus to its northern neighbors of Cappadocia, Pontus and Bithynia. In brief, Tarsus was a cosmopolitan city. On its streets could be seen sailors and merchantmen from many parts of the world, variously dressed and representing their diverse cultures.

Even though Saul was reared in a Jewish home and environment, he was also exposed to the Gentile world from the very beginning of his life. As he grew up he doubtless went to school at his own synagogue, but after school hours some of his friends and playmates would have been from Gentile homes. Also, assuming that his father was a tentmaker and that Saul worked as an apprentice in the shop, they would have come into contact many times with Gentile people who purchased their merchandise. Lasting impressions are made on young minds, and one of the impressions made on Saul was that many of the Gentiles, although not versed in the torah, were also good and kind people, "having God's law written on their hearts" (Rom 2:15).

Tarsus held another advantage for the young Saul. Located there was one of the great universities, close in rank with the universities at Athens and Alexandria. Indeed, some held it to be even superior to those at Athens and Alexandria, though not so prestigious. Students came to the university of Tarsus from many parts of the empire. Here one might study such subjects as natural science, astronomy, mathematics, languages, rhetoric, and philosophy. Tarsus was especially noted for its Stoic philosophers. One of its greatest, an elderly man when Saul was a growing boy, was Athenodorus, an esteemed citizen, who left behind many wise writings. He had been an instructor of Augustus in his younger years. It is entirely possible that Saul, being the student that he was, broadened his knowledge by reading from some of these philosophers or hearing them speak. It was inevitable that he would have been exposed to their influence.

In addition, Tarsus was the scene of the Roman games. Athletes came from far and wide to participate. People took as much interest in these games as we might take today in a Super Bowl football game or a soccer match. Doubtless, Saul attended some of these events. We can imagine that his father, for all his Pharisaic strictness, bent a little at this point to attend these notable events;

in the mind's eye, we can see father and son seated together in the grandstands. It was here that Saul secured some of his most telling athletic illustrations which appeared in his epistles in later years.

Parentage and Early Training

Saul was fortunate in his parentage. For one thing, he was born a Roman citizen which carried with it not only a certain honor and status but also certain rights and safeguards. Being a Roman citizen, he was free to travel anywhere in the empire. He could never be scourged and never be imprisoned without right to a trial. Further, if he was not satisfied with the judgment meted out, he could appeal directly to the emperor who was supposed to have at heart the welfare of the humblest citizen. We are not told how Saul's father acquired Roman citizenship. It may be that he received it in return for some civic service which he rendered. On the other hand he may have inherited it at birth just as Saul did (Acts 22:28). It is sufficient to say that Saul was fortunate to be born a Roman citizen, a fact which was to prove highly beneficial in later years.

From a religious standpoint also, he was fortunate in his parentage, for he was born into a pious God-fearing home. His parents were Pharisees of the strictest order. He later describes himself as having been "circumcised on the eighth day, of the people of Israel, of the tribe of Benjamin, a Hebrew born of Hebrews, as to the law a Pharisee" (Phil 3:4–5). He could be proud of his heritage.

It is not difficult to visualize the strictness of his parental discipline. Religion was not a once-a-week occasion but a vital part of family life. The Jewish rites were strictly observed in the home and in the synagogue. From an early age he was nurtured in the scriptures, reading them from the Greek translation, the Septuagint, learning the stories passed down for generations about his ancestry, and committing many of the passages to memory. Abraham, Sarah, Isaac, Rebecca, Jacob, Esau, Elijah, David, Jeremiah, and many others became familiar figures to him. When he started to the synagogue school, the scriptures were the main textbook, only now, in addition to the Greek translation, he learned to read them in their original language, Hebrew.

His Jewish upbringing made a profound impression on him and made him a debtor to heritage for which he was forever grateful. As evidence, consider the following passage:

I am speaking the truth in Christ, I am not lying; my
conscience bears me witness in the Holy Spirit, that I
have great sorrow and unceasing anguish in my heart.
For I could wish that I myself were accursed and cut off
from Christ for the sake of my brethren, my kinsmen by
race. They are Israelites, and to them belong the sonship,
the glory, the covenants, the giving of the law, the worship, and the promises; to them belong the patriarchs,
and of their race, according to the flesh, is the Christ
(Rom 9:1–5).

Learning a Trade

Every Jewish boy was supposed to learn a trade. While we
cannot be absolutely certain of this, it is reasonable to think that
Saul's father was most likely a tentmaker and the young boy grew
up learning the same trade. Tarsus was noted for its industries of
the weaving of linen and the making of tents. In any case, we
know that at some point Saul learned the trade of tentmaking and
that it was by this that he supported himself in later years. It is
likely that Saul's father had a weaving operation connected to his
shop. The cloth could have been woven from wool, or camels'
hair, or some combination. We are told that in this area there
were also herds of a certain breed of goat which bore a kind of
fleece suitable for making tents, curtains and hangings. Tents
could be made in many different sizes and styles according to the
desire of the customer. Of course, the cutting and stitching were
done by hand. It was an art form.

From Son of the Law to Rabbi

We can assume that at the age of twelve he became a "son of
the law." On the sabbath nearest his twelfth birthday, he would
have been asked certain questions before the elders of the synagogue to test his knowledge of the scriptures and of the Jewish
religion, and during the worship service he would have read one
of the scripture lessons from the Hebrew scroll. The rabbi would
have had some complimentary and encouraging words to say to
him and then would have presented him with a "son of the law"
certificate. How proud his parents must have been of him! From
this time forward, he was a responsible adult.

Many Jewish boys, having attained the status of "son of the
law," discontinued their formal training at this point, but not Saul.

For as long as he could remember, he had had in his mind the dream that someday he would like to become a rabbi. In this ambition he was encouraged by his parents. So he continued his studies under the leadership of the local rabbi until such time as he would have the opportunity to attend a rabbinical school. We can picture the rabbi making assignments of certain scripture passages to be studied and then later the two sitting down together to discuss the lessons which might be drawn from them. Not only was the literal meaning of a passage sought, but its symbolic or hidden meaning as well. Interpretation sometimes took the form of allegory. Increasingly, Saul showed his astuteness as an interpreter of the scriptures.

At the Feet of Gamaliel

We cannot be absolutely sure of chronology, but at some point in his early manhood, possibly around the age of fourteen or fifteen, a new door of opportunity opened to him. Without question, the most renowned Jewish scholar and teacher of that generation was Gamaliel, in Jerusalem. To sit at his feet was considered one of the greatest privileges anyone could have. The local rabbi at Tarsus perhaps had a hand in encouraging Saul to make his application and possibly had written a letter of reference to accompany the application. The application and letter were hand-carried by someone who was making a pilgrimage to Jerusalem to celebrate the Passover. In due time, when he returned, he had Gamaliel's letter of acceptance. Congratulations came to Saul from the entire Jewish community at Tarsus. They were proud to think that a son of their synagogue would have so singular an opportunity as to study under such an esteemed scholar.

Gamaliel represented the liberal wing of Jewish thought. At the time there were two opposing schools of interpretation of the scriptures. The one was known as the school of Shammai, and the other the school of Hillel. Both of these scholars were deceased, but their pupils carried on their traditions. Those of the school of Shammai represented the ultra-conservative wing. They insisted on the most literal interpretation of the scriptures and the strictest adherence to all the minute details of religious observance. The followers of Hillel, on the other hand, were more liberal in their interpretation of the scriptures and in their religious practices. One case in point concerned Gentile proselytes. The followers of Shammai barred them altogether; Jews alone were

God's people and had salvation. But the followers of Hillel welcomed Gentile converts as being also among the enlightened and saved.

Gamaliel was the grandson of "the great Hillel." He was a noted scholar and teacher in his own right and continued the broader outlook of this school. He was a gentle man with broad sympathies. Luke tells us that he "was held in honor by all the people" (Acts 5:34). At the time, when the early disciples were under persecution and some of the apostles were on trial before the Sanhedrin, while some were clamoring for blood, it was Gamaliel who calmed them down with his sound advice that there be no shedding of blood. He argued: "If this plan or undertaking is of men, it will fail; but if it be of God, you will not be able to overthrow them. You might even be found opposing God" (Acts 5:38–39).

Another example of Gamaliel's liberal views is seen in the fact that he believed it proper to read from Greek writers as well as Jewish, on the ground that truth is where one finds it. Of course his students were encouraged to broaden their knowledge in this realm also. Such liberalism was contrary to the school of Shammai where it was taught that it was proper to read only from the scriptures and other Jewish writers. Still another example of Gamaliel's liberal stance was found in his advocacy of laws and proceedings regarding divorce in favor of protecting the rights of women, who could claim few rights at best.

The esteem with which Gamaliel was held is further evidenced in the fact that to honor him the Sanhedrin established a new degree, or title, to be awarded only to the greatest of the great among scholars, the title of *rabban*, "our master, our great one." The first recipient was, of course, Gamaliel.

This was the man at whose feet the young man, Saul, was privileged to sit. In this school, instruction would have been given in Greek and Hebrew, though in ordinary conversations they spoke in Aramaic. Much of their time was spent in becoming thoroughly familiar with the scriptures and in memorizing vast portions. The instructor chose the passage of scripture for the day's special assignment. The students were encouraged to research what other scholars had said on the subject but also to give their own interpretation. Gamaliel encouraged the students to ask questions and to cross-examine one another. In the process Gamaliel would disclose what he considered to be the right or best interpretation. So it went day after day, except for weekends when students were free to attend one of the local synagogues. Saul likely attended the one made up of people who, like himself, had come from Cilicia (Acts 6:9).

During his stay in Jerusalem, Saul may have found room and board at the home of his sister, assuming that she was living in Jerusalem at this time. Of this we cannot be sure. We only know that at a later date he had a married sister there (Acts 23:16).

Return to Tarsus

How long his studies continued in Jerusalem cannot be stated with absolute certainty. The full course of training for the office of scribe covered a period, in some cases, of twelve years. The course of training for a rabbi was less than this. The time varied, beyond a minimum, from student to student, depending on whether a student felt that he had received all that a given school had to offer him. We cannot tell exactly how long Saul continued in Jerusalem as a student. A rough estimate might be ten years, at which time he would have been approximately twenty-three or twenty-four years of age. At this point he returned to Tarsus. We can well imagine how glad his parents were to have him back and how proud they were of him. We can assume further that the local rabbi would have been almost equally proud and would have had him in the pulpit to read from the scriptures and to give the exposition for the day.

But after a number of days at home, and having greeted all of his friends, we can surmise that Saul, with his restless, ambitious nature, would have been eager to get on with his life and to find a synagogue of his own where he might fill the role of rabbi for which he was now trained. There follow now several "silent years." It is interesting that both Jesus and Paul had their "silent years." With our mind's eye we can see him working diligently as a rabbi in some synagogue in Cilicia, conducting all of the worship services of the Jewish tradition, teaching youngsters just as he himself had been taught as a youth, continuing to read and study the scriptures, and growing in the grace and favor of the people to whom he ministered.

Saul, the Persecutor

However, even in a good situation, after a reasonable time, one can reach a state of mind of "mission accomplished." Saul began to have strong feelings that he should move on. It was not so much that he was dissatisfied with his present situation as he had a desire to move closer to the center of things, where the real action was taking place. It was in Jerusalem that the important decisions were made affecting Judaism. Saul realized that sooner or later he must move there if he was to make his own significant contribution. Having made his decision, he bade fond farewells to his friends and family in Cilicia and moved back to Jerusalem.

The New "Heresy"

It was a time of unrest and conflict between the Jewish authorities and the disciples of Jesus. The disciples were blatantly disregarding the instructions of the Sanhedrin that they desist from teaching in the name of Jesus (Acts 4:19–20; 5:27–29). Saul at first listened from the sidelines. But he was never one to remain uninvolved for long. His sentiments were clearly on the side of traditional Judaism.

To Saul and to many others reared in the Jewish tradition, the new teaching about Jesus was heresy. Worse than that, it was blasphemy! The disciples were teaching that Jesus, who died on a cross, was the promised messiah and Son of God. What a caricature this was of the traditional Jewish hope of one to sit on David's throne, one who would establish justice in the earth, and before whom kings would bow. What a far cry the cross was from this! The very fact that he had died on a cross was positive proof that the curse of God was upon him, for in the law it is written, "Cursed is everyone who hangs upon a tree" (Dt 21:23; Gal 3:13).

Saul and others with him felt that the sooner this aberration of Judaism was stamped out the better. But what to do about it was the question. The heresy seemed to be spreading like a brush fire, and the more they tried to stamp it out, the more it spread. For one thing, these people met in one another's homes, yet they frequented the synagogues where they openly avowed their cause, leading many of the simple-minded astray. They were teaching that Jesus was the messiah, not in spite of his suffering, but because he suffered, thus fulfilling the scriptures, citing Isaiah 53 in particular. They were saying that Jesus was the lamb of God who offered himself as a sacrifice in atonement for man's sins.

The Witness of Stephen

One of their most ardent spokesmen and debaters was Stephen, "a man full of faith and of the Holy Spirit," who was selected by the church as one of the first deacons. Regarding his debating ability, we read:

> Then some of those who belonged to the synagogue of the Freedmen (as it was called), and of the Cyrenians, and of the Alexandrians, and of those from Cilicia and Asia, arose and disputed with Stephen. But they could not withstand the wisdom and the Spirit with which he spoke (Acts 6:9–10).

We cannot but wonder if perchance Saul was among those from Cilicia who debated with Stephen and were bested in their arguments. Probably at this point he was only a listener.

We cannot go so far as to say that Saul was among those who stooped to secure false witnesses against Stephen, but he was present at the trial before the Sanhedrin and at the stoning. Where else did Luke get such precise information about the trial and subsequent execution? Luke records: "And gazing at him, all who sat in the council saw that his face was like the face of an angel" (Acts 6:15). Was this not drawn from Saul's memory? Further details are given of the stoning:

> And as they were stoning Stephen, he prayed, "Lord Jesus, receive my spirit." And he knelt down and cried with a loud voice, "Lord, do not hold this sin against them." And when he had said this, he fell asleep (Acts 7:59–60).

The entire account carries the strong suggestion that it comes from one who had been an eye-witness. This is further corroborated by the statement: "And the witnesses laid down their garments at the feet of a young man named Saul" (Acts 7:58).

"And Saul was consenting to his death" (Acts 8:1). The consent led to further involvement. He was never one to do things halfway. He was into the conflict now, doubtless with plenty of encouragement from others about him who felt as he did that this heresy, which had attached itself to Judaism, must be surgically removed. Quickly and willingly he rose from just one in the ranks to a top position of leadership. He found that he had plenty of support from the chief priests and from many members of the Sanhedrin, despite the wise and more tolerant advice which Gamaliel had given earlier when he had warned against the shedding of blood. The intensity of his zeal against the disciples is stated repeatedly:

> But Saul laid waste the church, and entering house after house he dragged off men and women and committed them to prison (Acts 8:3).

> I persecuted this Way to the death, binding and delivering to prison both men and women (Acts 22:4).

> I myself was convinced that I ought to do many things in opposing the name of Jesus of Nazareth. And I did so in Jerusalem; I not only shut up many of the saints in prison, by authority from the chief priests, but when they were put to death I cast my vote against them. And I punished them often in all the synagogues and tried to make them blaspheme; and in raging fury against them, I persecuted them even to foreign cities (Acts 26:9–11).

> For you have heard of my former life in Judaism, how I persecuted the church of God violently and tried to destroy it (Gal 1:13).

The quotation from Acts 26 suggests that Saul's zeal had been rewarded by his being made a member of the Sanhedrin, now able to cast his own vote against the disciples. If Saul's conscience bothered him in all of this, as might be inferred from his later reference about it hurting "to kick against the goads," he sought to evade or assuage his feelings by yet fiercer persecutions. Thus activity took the place of reflection and repentance. He would not allow himself enough time to even consider that he might be on a wrong course in his hot pursuit of eradicating this menace to Judaism.

If Saul's intent was to create havoc among the new sect, he was highly successful, for many disciples were uprooted from their homes and settled elsewhere throughout Judea and Samaria and other parts. Some settled in Damascus. Some went as far north as Antioch. But if his intent was to stamp out the movement, he was failing miserably. For wherever these refugees went, they carried their insidious faith with them and formed new nests of operation. Philip was stirring up things in Samaria where it was reported that he was making new converts with amazing success (Acts 8:1–40). However, Saul would not admit defeat; he would press relentlessly on:

> But Saul, still breathing threats and murder against the disciples of the Lord, went to the high priest and asked him for letters to the synagogues at Damascus, so that if he found any belonging to the Way, men or women, he might bring them bound to Jerusalem (Acts 9:1–2).

The Damascus Road Encounter

There are three accounts of Saul's conversion as he journeyed on the road to Damascus. The first is told by Luke in the third person (Acts 9). The second and third are related by Paul himself as he told his story, first to the people of Jerusalem in the presence of the Roman tribune (Acts 22), and subsequently to King Agrippa in the presence of the Roman governor, Festus (Acts 26). As we examine these three accounts and place them side by side, there are certain differences, yet they are not discrepancies but only variations of details and of a minor nature. The great truth that stands out is that Saul, journeying from Jerusalem to Damascus and almost there, suddenly and unexpectedly encountered the risen Christ, who spoke to him.

Let us try to visualize the setting and the circumstances. Damascus was approximately one hundred and forty miles from Jerusalem. The last part of the journey would have been across desert terrain. Saul and his armed companions were traveling on foot into their fifth day, a hard journey. The fact that they were pressing on at noonday indicates something of the intensity with which Saul was pursuing his purpose, for in the east most travelers would have called a halt and sought relief from the heat of the noonday sun. But it was noonday, Paul tells us, when suddenly there shone from heaven a great light, above the brightness of the sun, whereupon Saul and those with him fell to the earth.

It was then that Saul heard a voice speaking to him in the Hebrew tongue, "Saul, Saul, why do you persecute me? It hurts you to kick against the goads." Those traveling with Saul saw the light, but either they did not hear the voice, or if they heard it did not understand it. In any event they probably did not know the Hebrew language. Saul responded, "Who are you, Lord?" And he answered, "I am Jesus whom you are persecuting." Saul said, "What shall I do, Lord?" And he said, "Rise, and go into Damascus, and there you will be told all that is appointed for you to do." Rising to his feet, Saul found that he could not see because of the brightness of the light that had blinded him. So those who were with him took him by the hand and led him into Damascus. What a comedown! Saul, the raging persecutor, being led by the hand into Damascus!

Many writers have tried to analyze more precisely just what could have taken place in the experience of Saul. Some writers begin with the assumption that the accounts cannot be taken at face value and Saul could not really have encountered the risen Christ. Speculation goes on from there. For example, regarding the blinding light, it is conjectured that this may have been a sudden bolt of lightning at close quarters. We are told that such a thing is not uncommon in that part of the world as the cold layers of air coming off the snow-capped peaks of Mount Hermon sweep down and meet the rising hot air from the desert. If it were a bolt of lightning, it might also account for the temporary blindness of Saul. But what of the others traveling with Saul? Would not they, too, have been blinded, at least some of them? Some writers have suggested that his physical affliction, of which he speaks later (2 Cor 12:7), may have been epilepsy and on the Damascus road he experienced an epileptic seizure. However, it is futile for us to speculate what happened in terms of naturalistic causes, or in terms of psychology or physiology. We simply do not know.

To Saul it was nothing other than an encounter with the risen Christ. To him the experience was real, as real as anything that had ever happened to him, and it turned his life around "about face." At the same time we should avoid the other extreme of being dogmatic as to what form the vision took. Was it an outward vision which he saw with his physical eyes, or an inner vision which was impressed upon his mind? A passage in Galatians leads one to think that the vision was inward: "But when he who had set me apart before I was born, and had called me through his grace, was pleased to reveal his Son *in* me . . ." (Gal 1:15–16). It must be borne in mind also that Saul was the only one of the company who saw the vision.

Also, the voice! As we have noted, either those traveling with him did not hear the voice or it was inarticulate to them. The accounts are not clear on this point. However, to Saul, the voice was distinct, "in the Hebrew tongue," and left no doubt in his mind what he should do. He was not to return to Jerusalem, as one might have expected, but was to proceed to Damascus and there await further orders.

It should be noted here that Saul had other visions of the Lord. Later, after he had returned to Jerusalem and was trying to make his witness there, while in the temple he had a vision of the Lord who told him to depart, for those in Jerusalem would not receive his witness; instead, the Lord had plans to send him far away to the Gentiles (Acts 22:17–21). At a much later date in Jerusalem, after he had been arrested following a riot by the Jews, the account says, "The following night the Lord stood by him and said, 'Take courage, for as you have testified about me at Jerusalem, so you must bear witness also at Rome' " (Acts 23:11). There was also a vision during his voyage to Rome (Acts 27:21–26). Did these visions differ in kind from the one on the Damascus road? We cannot tell. But we do know that the one on the Damascus road had priority. It was this one which wrought such a radical change in him, transforming him from a persecutor of the faith into its strongest proponent.

Significance of the Encounter

What was the significance of this vision for Saul? Essentially four things, although doubtless he did not stop to analyze them and set them in order, as we do here, particularly since they all overlap and coalesce.

(1) *First and foremost, the vision meant for Saul that Jesus was alive.* The resurrection stories which the disciples had been affirming and circulating were really true! Up to this time Saul had been incredulous. But now, as suddenly as the flash of light, his defenses went down, and he was confronted by a living Lord. Theoretically, in his question "Who are you, Lord?" he was asking for identity. In fact, the identity was contained in the question. He was confronted by Jesus Christ, the one whom the disciples had been proclaiming as "Lord." With this fact firmly established in his mind, everything to the contrary had to change. For him the resurrection became the one fact by which everything else had to be measured.

Of course the cross became central in his thought too, but even the cross would have been of no effect apart from the resurrection. This is the point that he makes later to the Corinthians: "If Christ has not been raised, your faith is futile and you are still in your sins. . . . If in this life we who are in Christ have only hope, we are of all men most to be pitied" (1 Cor 15:17–19).

(2) *Second, his vision showed him that the course he had been pursuing was wrong.* Stephen and the other disciples whom he had been persecuting were right after all, and he was wrong. Jesus was the messiah, just as they had been proclaiming. He was the messiah, not in spite of his suffering, but because he suffered. Many passages in the scriptures were now to come to light and take on new meaning. The scriptures, together with the dreams and hopes of Israel, found their fulfillment in Jesus.

(3) *Third, his vision led him to the conclusion that the crucifixion, far from being the curse of God, was the supreme act of his grace.* The cross, together with the resurrection, was to become central in his thought and in his preaching. The cross became the proof of God's love and the supreme sacrifice for the sins of his people. Salvation was to be had, not by self-righteousness, or obedience to the law, but by grace and grace alone, and the new covenant between God and his people was sealed by the very blood of his Son, Jesus.

(4) *Fourth, his vision was linked directly to his commission to apostleship.* He had seen the Lord and had been commissioned by him just as truly as the other apostles in their own experiences. If ever his apostleship was questioned, as it was to be, he always fell back to the fact that his commission was from Christ himself. In Galatians, he begins by reminding his readers of his divine appointment to apostleship: "Paul an apostle, not from men nor through man, but through Jesus Christ and God the Father, who raised him from the dead . . ." (Gal 1:1). To the Corinthians he writes: "Am I not free? Am I not an apostle? Have I not seen Jesus our Lord?" (1 Cor 9:1). Whereas he always sought for peace and unity in the church, nevertheless if his apostolic authority was called in question, he appealed to the undeniable fact that it was Jesus Christ himself who had called and commissioned him; to him he owed his supreme allegiance.

The Ministry of Ananias

Returning to the Damascus scene, how we wish that we might know more about that saint of Damascus named Ananias. Scripture is silent as to his background. Was he one of those disciples who had been driven from Jerusalem by the tempestuous persecution under Saul? So far as Luke's account is concerned, he is like a character in a play who comes upon the stage, does his part exceedingly well, and then makes his exit, not to be heard from again.

Events do not take place in a vacuum, and God's ministries often come through other people. Luke tells us that there was a second vision, this one to Ananias who was to be God's agent in ministry to Saul in a time of desperate need. In his vision, Ananias was commanded by the Lord to go to such and such a house where Saul was staying and to lay his hands upon him, that he might receive his sight. Ananias reminded the Lord of the great evils done by Saul and of his mission of death to Damascus, but the Lord answered him, "Go, for he is a chosen instrument of mine to carry my name before the Gentiles and kings and the sons of Israel; for I will show him how much he must suffer for the sake of my name" (Acts 9:15–16).

We can imagine the trepidation with which Ananias obeyed his orders. What would he say to this man? What kind of reception would he have? How would he call such a man to repentance? By the time he arrived and knocked on the door, the Holy Spirit had done his work. When Ananias was ushered into the presence of Saul, he found him praying, deeply disturbed and uncertain. The first words of Ananias were, "Brother Saul . . ." What a warm greeting to one who had been the arch-enemy and had done such great harm. How the words must have warmed the heart of Saul. No recrimination! Not even a call to repentance! No need for that to a man on his knees! What Saul needed now was comfort, assurance, and direction. These Ananias brought him in the name of the Lord.

First Ananias laid his hands upon him and prayed that he might regain his sight, and immediately, so it seemed, his sight began to return. Saul told Ananias about his experience on the Damascus road and asked that he might be received into this new faith. It may have seemed a bit premature to Ananias, but who was he to resist the working of the Holy Spirit? So gathering a small group of disciples about them, they made their way to the banks of the Abana river where Ananias proceeded to baptize Saul with a baptism he would always remember and refer to repeatedly. It was like death and resurrection. It was a dying to the old self and rising again to a new life.

Being always a man of action, one who believed that convictions should be matched with deeds, Saul felt that he should begin at once to make his testimony in the synagogues of Damascus, to tell his story of what he had experienced and how he had been led to the conclusion that Jesus was indeed the Messiah. What a disappointment it must have been to him to find that his hearers were skeptical. That a change had come over him was evident, but his message did not penetrate them. After all, they had been in the Judaistic mold a long time. He had seen a vision, so he testified, but no revelation had come to them. After some days, it seemed to him that all he was doing was creating resistance and making enemies as he pitted his arguments against theirs. So it had been in the days of Stephen when Saul was on the other side. He found himself using the same arguments that Stephen had used and the same scriptures, but his words were falling on deaf ears. The door in Damascus seemed closed, at least for the time being.

Journey to Arabia

The official record in the book of Acts becomes somewhat sketchy at this point concerning Saul. Luke, the historian, turns his attention to the contribution of other leaders in the church, notably to the apostle Peter. This period in the life of Saul has to be pieced together in jigsaw fashion with bits of information from the epistles supplementing the account in Acts. From Galatians we learn that he next spent some time in Arabia—"three years," he says, although as they then reckoned time this could mean only parts of three years. The account in Galatians reads:

> But when he who had set me apart before I was born, and had called me through his grace, was pleased to reveal his Son in me, in order that I might preach him among the Gentiles, I did not confer with flesh and blood, nor did I go up to Jerusalem to those who were apostles before me, but I went away into Arabia; and again I returned to Damascus. Then after three years I went up to Jerusalem to visit Cephas, and remained with him fifteen days . . . (Gal 1:15–18).

Things had been happening fast and furiously for Saul since his vision on the Damascus road, and even though Ananias and others had been of immense help, he needed time to be alone to sort things out and to think through their implications. Where should he go? To some desert place. By desert, scripture does not necessarily mean a windswept, sandy, barren landscape. Nor does it mean a place completely depopulated. It may mean simply a place where the population is sparse. Saul decided to make the long trek to Arabia, some four hundred miles to the south.

Where in Arabia? We are not told, but since Arabia included Mount Sinai (also known as Mount Horeb), where both Moses and Elijah received their inspiration, it is natural to suppose that this was the spot sought out by Saul. There, he recalled the best in his heritage and realized that he, too, was standing on holy ground. He recalled how God had spoken to Moses amid the thunder and lightning, and how he had spoken to Elijah in a still small voice. In just as real a way, if not more so, God had spoken to him on the Damascus road. He must now try to reconcile heritage with present revelation and move with obedience into the future.

The law, for all its worth, had not brought him peace and contentment. With its legalistic demands it left him always with a sense of failure, for no one can perfectly fulfill its requirements. No one, try as he may, can perfectly measure up to the righteousness which God requires. He had appreciated the exposition of the scriptures under Gamaliel, but in practice the legalistic system brought him no real satisfaction or joy, because he always found himself on the debit side. By contrast he had never known such overwhelming peace and contentment, such joy and sense of freedom, as he had experienced since becoming a disciple of Jesus. In addition, ever since his baptism, he had had a deep sense of the indwelling presence of the Holy Spirit, such as he had not known under Judaism. Here at Sinai, he began to wrestle with the relationship between law and grace, which he would develop later into the formal treatises of Galatians and Romans.

As he stood on one of the peaks of Sinai and looked out over the wide vistas of space, the presence of God seemed very real. In his heart he felt that God was speaking to him with a commission and accompanying promises clear and certain: "I have chosen you to bear my name to many peoples. Fear not! Surely I will be with you. I will strengthen you, I will help you, yea, I will uphold you with the right hand of my righteousness."

Where and how God planned to use him, he did not know. He only knew that he must now return, in the strength of the Lord, in the power of the Spirit, to bear his witness, whether his hearers

would respond or forebear. The word of God in him was a consuming fire!

Return to Damascus

He returned to Damascus where he found simple lodging.
For financial support he made contact with a tentmaking firm that
agreed to hire him. Whereas tentmaking was his means of liveli-
hood, his main vocation was in witnessing to his faith. Night by
night and sabbath by sabbath, he attempted to bear his witness in
a positive and constructive way, both in the synagogues and in
private homes, but in the synagogues he met with a cold reception. In fact, there began to be open hostility toward him and
threats against his life. It was no longer safe for him to go out alone
at night. His friends became concerned for his security.

He had mentioned that he had hopes of returning soon to
Jerusalem to visit the apostles and disciples there. His enemies
picked up this information and made arrangements to have the
gates of the city watched day and night so that the moment he
emerged beyond the city walls he would be accosted and killed.
Thus Saul, the former persecutor, found himself persecuted. The
result of this immediate situation was that his friends "took him by
night and let him down over the wall, lowering him in a basket"
(Acts 9:25; 2 Cor 11:32–33). Thus, for the moment at least, he
escaped the hands of his enemies.

Return to Jerusalem

He made his way to Jerusalem. Did he travel, in reverse, the
same route along which he and the temple soldiers had come
some three years before? If so, did he pause at the place of his
vision with recollection and reflection? We are not told. Upon his
arrival in Jerusalem he made his way to his sister's home where he
was always welcome, even though she did not understand what
was going on in his mind. He inquired about when and where the
next meeting of the disciples was to take place and made his way
there. He did not know what kind of reception he would receive
but he soon found out. They were skeptical of the genuineness of
his faith and were afraid of him. They had heard that he who once
persecuted the church was now witnessing to the faith which he
had persecuted, but this was not totally convincing; they had
witnessed too much suffering at his hands in days gone by to

readily accept a turn-around. But Barnabas, big-hearted Barnabas, whose name means "son of consolation," took him under tow and brought him to the apostles where he convincingly persuaded them of the genuineness of his conversion (Acts 9:27).

So he went in and out among the disciples in Jerusalem and witnessed to his faith, "preaching boldly in the name of the Lord" (Acts 9:29). Then he tried the synagogues, but met with the same hostility that he had encountered in Damascus. As there had been threats against his life in Damascus, so it was in Jerusalem. It was not that he was afraid to die, but was it for this that he had received the vision on the Damascus road? And was it for this that assurances had been given in Arabia? He tells us that while he was in the temple praying, he fell into a trance and had a vision in which the Lord said to him, "Make haste and get quickly out of Jerusalem, because they will not accept your testimony about me." Saul answered, "Lord, they themselves know that in every synagogue I imprisoned and beat those who believed in thee. And when the blood of Stephen thy witness was shed, I also was standing by and approving, and keeping the garments of those who killed him." But the Lord said to him, "Depart, for I will send you far away to the Gentiles" (Acts 22:17–21). Thus Saul was convinced that God had other purposes for him than to die at this point, and that it was not cowardly to leave the scene of danger.

The historical account itself is brief at this point. Luke simply records that when the brethren knew of the threats against Saul's life, they brought him down to Caesarea and sent him off to Tarsus (Acts 9:30).

Ministry in Cilicia and Syria

What kind of reception did his parents give him upon his arrival in Tarsus? No doubt they had heard rumors about the changes that had taken place in their son's life as he had turned from being an esteemed rabbi to a persecutor of the new sect. They had found it hard to believe at first that their son could be a persecutor of anyone, for whatever reasons, until the rumors were confirmed. Then it was harder still to accept. Later, reports came of a complete turn-around. Perhaps Saul himself wrote them about his change in faith. However, upon his arrival, they were not prepared for the radical change which they found in his theological thinking. Of course they welcomed him lovingly as their son, and they listened to him for long hours. Yet, it is often true that those hardest to witness to effectively are members of one's own household. It is likely that they listened respectfully to their learned son, but remained firmly entrenched in their Pharisaic faith. One wonders if a part of Paul's agony for Israel in Romans 9–11 is a reflection of his own household.

Here, in Luke's history of the church, Saul drops out of sight for a period of some six or seven years. We cannot be absolutely precise as to chronology. During these years we can follow him in our thoughts as he visits various synagogues in Cilicia and Syria, making his witness "to the Jews first." However, as he had opportunity, he spoke with Gentiles also and sometimes felt that his witness to them was better received than by his own people. We can imagine, too, that as he had opportunity, he formed small groups of disciples to meet in one another's homes to study the scriptures, to pray, and to worship, after the manner of the disciples in Judea.

There are three clues given in scripture as to what Saul was doing during those six or seven years. The first is from Paul himself in his brief autobiographical sketch in Galatians where he relates what happened with him after he left Jerusalem, after his life had been threatened and his friends had taken him to Caesarea and seen him aboard a ship bound for Tarsus (Acts 9:30). He writes: "Then I went into the regions of Syria and Cilicia. And I was still not known by sight to the churches of Christ in Judea; they only heard it said, 'He who once persecuted us is now preaching the faith he once tried to destroy' " (Gal 1:21–23).

The second clue follows what is known as the Jerusalem Council as recorded in the fifteenth chapter of Acts. The action of the council resulted in a letter addressed to the churches. The greeting reads: "The brethren, both the apostles and the elders, to the brethren who are of the Gentiles in Antioch and Syria and Cilicia, greeting . . ." (Acts 15:23).

The third clue comes at the beginning of the second missionary journey. The account reads: "But Paul chose Silas and departed, being commended by the brethren to the grace of the Lord. And he went through Syria and Cilicia, strengthening the churches" (Acts 15:40–41).

How had these churches in Syria and Cilicia come into being? We are not told, but it is reasonable to think that Saul of Tarsus had had a hand in organizing some of them during those years when he was minister-at-large in the regions of Cilicia and Syria.

Ministry at Antioch

Meanwhile, important developments were taking place in Antioch in Syria. Following the death of Stephen many of the disciples, under persecution, dispersed to various places. Phoenicia, Cyprus, and Antioch are cited in particular (Acts 11:19). Although uprooted from their native soil, the disciples took their religion with them wherever they went and thus the gospel spread. In the beginning the disciples were witnessing to Jews only, mostly in the synagogues. But in Antioch some of the disciples from the Greek-speaking world, namely from Cyrene and Cyprus, began witnessing to the Greeks (Gentiles) as well, with considerable success (Acts 11:20–21).

There were many Gentile people who had grown weary of the Greek and Roman gods and goddesses and the immorality associated with their shrines. In Antioch itself, the chief shrine was to the Greek goddess Daphne. Some of the Gentiles, looking for a religion of high moral standards as well as hope, had turned to Judaism. They were in two classes. The *Godfearers*, as they were called, were those who merely attended the synagogue services. There were others, a few, who went all the way and subjected themselves to the rite of circumcision; these were known as *proselytes*. Most of the Gentiles who attached themselves to Judaism were the Godfearers who merely attended the synagogue for worship and study and participated in the Jewish festivals.

These disciples from Cyrene and Cyprus began holding services in their homes, apart from the synagogue, with increasing success. They had the same scriptures as the Jewish community except that these writings had been translated into Greek, called the Septuagint. The disciples taught that the scriptures had been fulfilled in the historic person of Jesus Christ, who had been crucified, but who had been raised from the dead and exalted to the right hand of God, and who during his earthly ministry had taught an even higher standard of morality than Moses. It was a religion which stressed faith in God, repentance, forgiveness of sins, salvation, and eternal life. It also stressed expressing one's faith in works of charity. These home gatherings developed an intimate, close-knit fellowship.

As word spread of these gatherings, more and more Gentiles responded, with the result that the Gentile element of the church was growing faster than its Jewish counterpart. This was a new phenomenon. Word of this situation reached the apostles in Jerusalem where it caused some concern. They dispatched Barnabas to Antioch to investigate. They could not have chosen a better emissary. With his broadminded and compassionate spirit, he saw the Lord's hand at work in this new development among the Gentiles (Acts 11:22–23).

Barnabas doubtless sent a report back to the apostles and elders in Jerusalem telling them about how he had found the grace of God at work among the Gentiles, and that he had decided to stay a while longer to assist in this growing work among them. Most of the Gentile converts, while sincere, were woefully ignorant of the scriptures and needed instruction and nurture.

It was at this point that Barnabas remembered just the man uniquely qualified to assist with this venture. He recalled also how Saul had shared with him his vision that the Lord was calling him to work among the Gentiles (Acts 9:30; 22:21). So Barnabas himself went to Tarsus in search of Saul, and when he had found him he persuaded him that the Lord had a work for him to do in Antioch. We might say that it was Barnabas who rescued Saul from obscurity, although he was doing a fine work where he was and brought him back into the mainstream. Antioch was to become one of the great centers of the church. But it was not Barnabas alone who made the choice; it was the leading of the Holy Spirit.

For a year or more Barnabas and Saul worked among the Gentile disciples in Antioch "and taught a large company of people." We have to read between the lines to realize what a tremendous asset Saul was in this work and how well equipped he was for it. It is of interest to note that it was in Antioch that the disciples were for the first time called Christians (Acts 11:26).

Mission of Aid to Judea

About this time there was a severe famine in the region of Palestine and the disciples in Antioch determined to send relief to the brethren who lived in Judea. They reasoned that not only would they like to be of assistance, but that the act would be a gesture of good will from the Gentile segment of the church to their Jewish brethren. We can visualize Barnabas and Saul exhorting the disciples in Antioch to liberality. Each person was to give according to ability (Acts 11:29). That Barnabas and Saul had a leading hand in this project is suggested by the fact that they were the ones chosen to deliver the gift to the apostles and elders in Jerusalem. This would have been Saul's second visit to Jerusalem since his conversion. It had been some eight years since he had been in Jerusalem and some eleven years since his conversion.

A great deal had taken place during those intervening years, both in Saul's personal life and in the life of the church. Most of the apostles had departed from Jerusalem and were bearing their witness in various parts of the empire. King Herod Agrippa I, a grandson of Herod the Great, was ruler at the time of their visit. He had studied in Rome where at a young age he had become a friend of both Caius (Caligula) and Claudius and had ingratiated himself with them. He was rewarded bountifully. Partly through these friendships and partly through his own machinations he was made king of the northern part of Palestine, extending from Caesarea Philippi to Samaria, and then subsequently Samaria and Judea were added to his domain, so that he ruled a territory as large as that of Herod the Great and larger than Solomon's.

To favor the Jews and to add to his own prestige, he persecuted the Christians, killing James the son of Zebedee, the first apostolic martyr. He arrested Peter also, intending to execute him after the Passover season, but Peter experienced a miraculous rescue and disappeared from sight for a time (Acts 12:1–19). These were the political conditions at the time that Barnabas and Saul brought the gift from the Gentile Christians in Antioch to their Jewish brethren in Jerusalem. It was not the best of times to be sure—a famine in the land and persecution taking place under an arrogant, ruthless ruler. Yet the work of the Lord continued and, far from being stamped out, was growing. "But the word of God grew and multiplied" (Acts 12:24).

Return to Antioch

When Barnabas and Saul had completed their mission in Jerusalem, they returned to Antioch, taking with them John Mark, the cousin of Barnabas. John's home was in Jerusalem and was the meeting place of the early Christians. John had listened to Barnabas and Saul as they told their story about the work in Antioch. To John, Antioch sounded like a faraway place and the work exciting. After talking things over with his mother, he volunteered his assistance to Barnabas and Saul. His offer was accepted, and so begins the story of a young man who was to make his own significant contribution to the Christian church.

Commissioned by the Church

Once back in Antioch, Barnabas and Saul continued their work with the assistance of John Mark. For how long we do not know, but apparently not very long, because God had other plans for them. As some of the leaders in the church in Antioch were "worshiping the Lord and fasting," the Holy Spirit said, "Set apart for me Barnabas and Saul for the work to which I have called them" (Acts 13:2). Just how the Holy Spirit spoke to them we are not told, but they firmly believed that their decision was God's bidding. The main thrust of their decision was that the gospel was not private or provincial but was for the entire world. But how shall the world hear except there be those who are sent?

It was also the general consensus among those magnanimous Christians of Antioch that they should send their best. Who were better qualified for the task than Barnabas and Saul? It was truly the leading of the Holy Spirit. As soon as preparations could be made, a special service of ordination and commissioning was held, with fasting and prayer and the laying on of hands. Then, with deep emotion, with both joy and tears, they bade them farewell and sent them off, John Mark accompanying them. So being sent forth by the Holy Spirit, they went down to Seleucia, the seaport, and from there they sailed for Cyprus. The first missionary journey had begun.

We shall bring the biographical sketch to a halt at this point. To follow the apostle further through the details of his missionary career, the writing of his letters, his many trials and hardships, his imprisonment and trip to Rome, would take us afield from our present purpose. However, this much of his biography, as has been given, should help set the stage for us as we now consider his remarkable and compelling Christology, coming from one who had been the arch-enemy of the early church.

How did it happen that a contemporary of Jesus, who first looked upon him as a kind of charlatan and menace to true religion, could so change his mind as to believe and declare: "In him all the fullness of God was pleased to dwell"? Further, that this one who died on the cross, "God has highly exalted . . . and given him the name that is above every name"? To these questions we now turn our attention.

2

Pleroma—The "Fullness of God" in Jesus Christ

The Christology of St. Paul is possessed of that sublime and inexhaustible quality which is native to enduring truth. His loftiest descriptions of the Lord Jesus, far from having faded into obsolescence, still evoke our reflection, as they elude it, by their very greatness. They are still beyond us as of old; we can but throw out our minds at an infinite reality; and to the last the believing consciousness will vainly strive to know the depth and height beheld by the apostle in Christ Jesus as he wrote: "In him were all things created, in the heavens and the earth, things visible and things invisible . . . for in him dwelleth all the fullness of the Godhead bodily" (H.R. Mackintosh, *The Person of Jesus Christ*, p. 76).

We come now to consider Paul's lofty view of Christ, especially as we find it in the book of Colossians. Our procedure will be first to look at the pertinent passages in Colossians, then to examine the Colossian heresy with which Paul was contending, and finally to probe into the background of Paul's elevated language.

Two Preliminary Observations

Two preliminary observations need to be made at the outset as we consider Paul's view of Christ. These may seem obvious; nevertheless, they need to be stated.

(1) *First, there is Paul's firm grounding in monotheism.* Among the many contributions of Judaism to the world is the unconditional affirmation of monotheism. By Paul's time, monotheism was not so much taught as taken for granted in Jewish

circles. From infancy, every Jewish child was taught to recite the *Shema:* "Hear, O Israel, the Lord our God is one Lord . . ." (Dt 6:4). Every worship service in the synagogue included it.

Paul was fully aware of the polytheistic culture which surrounded him at every turn—the many altars in Athens, for example. Yet he himself remained firmly rooted in monotheism. To the Corinthians he wrote:

> For although there may be so-called gods in heaven or on earth—as indeed there are many "gods" and many "lords"—yet for us there is one God, the Father, from whom are all things and for whom we exist, and one Lord, Jesus Christ, through whom are all things and through whom we exist (1 Cor 8:5–6).

Yet Paul found no incompatibility between his belief in monotheism and his affirmation of the deity of Jesus Christ in the same context with God the Father. Frequently the two names occur in juxtaposition as the source of grace and peace. Take just one example:

> Grace to you and peace from God our Father and the Lord Jesus Christ (Rom 1:7).

In a similar way, in numerous places, Paul links Christ and the Holy Spirit, never to the point of identity but in closest correlation in their work. Again, a single example will suffice:

> But you are not in the flesh, you are in the Spirit, if the Spirit of God really dwells in you. Any one who does not have the spirit of Christ does not belong to him. But if Christ is in you, although your bodies are dead because of sin, your spirits are alive because of righteousness (Rom 8:9–10).

To be in the Spirit and to be in Christ are inseparable in experience.

The doctrine of the Trinity finds strong support on almost every page of Paul's epistles. Yet he found no inconsistency whatsoever between his faith in one God and his belief that this God manifests himself as sovereign Father, as Jesus Christ his Son, and as Holy Spirit, the life of God in persons.

(2) *The second observation to keep in mind as we contemplate Paul's lofty view of Jesus Christ is that he was fully cognizant of his humanity.* We might be prone to take this for granted, but when we consider the strange medley of beliefs which existed in Paul's day, it becomes less obvious.

We do not know whether Paul ever saw Jesus during his earthly lifetime. But that he knew about his earthly ministry, his crucifixion, and the claims made about him by his disciples is certain. It was those claims for the man Jesus who had died on a cross that became the basis for Paul's persecutions of the early disciples. There was never the least doubt in Paul's mind but that Jesus was an historical person. It was real blood that had been shed on the cross (Col 1:20). His life was no phantom-like existence, as the Docetists were to claim later.

It was this person, who was Paul's contemporary, for whom he now claimed the highest attributes and prerogatives which previously had been reserved for God alone.

The Locus Classicus

Although the divine nature of Jesus Christ is affirmed in many New Testament passages, and inferred throughout, one of the strongest and most profound statements is from St. Paul in the first chapter of Colossians. It was at Colossae that the full deity of Christ was being challenged by false teachers. We shall have more to say about the "Colossian heresy" later in this chapter. Here, it is sufficient to note that Paul's great statement concerning Christ was designed to voice the true faith of the church and to put an end to all such false teachings as would demote him from his full rank in the Godhead. The classical passage reads as follows:

> He (Christ) is the image of the invisible God, the first-born of all creation; for in him all things were created, in heaven and on earth, visible and invisible, whether thrones or dominions or principalities or authorities—all things were created through him and for him. He is before all things, and in him all things hold together. He is the head of the body, the church; he is the beginning, the first-born from the dead, that in everything he might be preeminent. For in him all the fullness of God was pleased to dwell, and through him to reconcile to himself

all things, whether on earth or in heaven, making peace
by the blood of his cross (Col 1:15–20).

As we examine this passage, we observe that Paul identifies
three relationships of Christ: to God, to creation, and to the
church.

(1) *His relationship to God.* "He is the image (*eikon*) of the
invisible God." An *eikon* was an exact reproduction of the likeness
of someone. Thus, a portrait of a person would be that person's
eikon, or a statue of a person would be his or her *eikon*. Paul was
saying that in Jesus Christ we have an exact representation and
manifestation of the invisible God.

Our thoughts travel naturally back to the Genesis creation
story where it is said that God created man in his own image. That
image became marred by sin. Through all the centuries since, the
image of God has been marred in man. But Paul affirms that in
Christ, the image of God was exhibited as a perfect likeness. The
image, lost in Adam, was restored in Christ.

(2) *His relationship to creation.* He is described as the "first-
born of all creation." The Greek term is *prototokos*. It can indeed
mean in some instances the first-to-be-born, within a time frame,
but not necessarily so. In Jewish usage it came to have a technical
sense of God's favored one. The first-born was the heir. He was
the one who had the priority, the first place in relationship. The
term was used of Israel in the sense of God's favored one. For
example, Moses was instructed to go to Pharaoh and to say to him,
"Thus says the Lord, 'Israel is my first-born son. Let my son go
that he may serve me' " (Ex 4:23–24).

It should be clearly understood that Paul's use of the word
does not mean that Christ was the first of created things. Indeed,
this is precluded in the statement which follows where it is em-
phatically declared that he is the source and agent in the creation
of "all things in heaven and on earth, visible and invisible. . . . He
is before all things, and in him all things hold together." Here
Paul affirms that Christ was preexistent to creation, that he was
God's agent in creation, and that in him all things hold together
(cohere).

The term "first-born" also came to have a messianic meaning.
In Psalm 89:27–28, God, in speaking of his servant, David, says:
"I will make him the first-born, the highest of the kings of earth.
My steadfast love I will keep for him forever, and my covenant
will stand firm for him." This passage was commonly interpreted

as messianic, a prophecy concerning the coming messiah. By Paul's time, the term first-born was equated with God's chosen one, the messiah.

(3) *His relationship to the church.* Three terms are used to describe Christ's relationship to the church.

First, "he is the *head* of the body, the church." This is one of Paul's favorite metaphors in portraying the relationship between Christ and his church. As the head directs the actions of the body, so Christ directs his church. But more than this, in Paul's time the head was regarded as the seat of life, unifying the different members into one organic whole. The body was totally dependent upon the head for coordination and for growth and development (see Col 2:19; Eph 4:15–16).

The second term describing Christ's relationship to the church is *"the beginning"* (*arche*). The English translation, "the beginning," does not do justice to the Greek. The Greek term means not only the beginning, but the origin, the first in rank, hence the leader. Christ is the origin of his church, first in rank, the leader.

The third term describing his relationship to the church is the phrase *"first-born from the dead."* The phrase "first-born from the dead" corresponds to "first-born of all creation," so that there is a parallelism between Christ's lordship over creation and his lordship over his new creation, the church. It is specifically the resurrection that demonstrates his sovereignty over death, his lordship of the church, and his universal preeminence (1:18).

The "Fullness of God" in Christ

What follows is undoubtedly one of the greatest and most profound statements in the New Testament concerning the person of Christ.

> For in him all the fullness (*pleroma*) of God was pleased to dwell" (1:19).

The structure of this verse in the Greek is complicated in that the name of God does not appear, but almost all commentators agree that it is implied. As the sentence stands in the Greek, the literal translation is: "For all the *pleroma* was pleased to dwell in him." Some translators find their way out of the dilemma by making God (implied) the subject, and the verse then reads: "For God was pleased to have all his fullness dwell in him" (New International Version).

Fortunately, the meaning of this verse is greatly aided by a very similar reading in the second chapter where the Godhead is clearly stated:

> For in him (Christ) the whole fullness (*pleroma*) of deity (*theotetos*) dwells bodily" (2:9).

This is a tremendous statement, that the "fullness of God" was manifested "in bodily form." It is in line with the statement made by the fourth evangelist: "And the Word (*Logos*) became flesh and dwelt among us, full of grace and truth" (Jn 1:14).

This great Christological section (Col 1:15–20) is climaxed by a statement regarding the redemptive work of Christ. It was God's pleasure that all of his fullness should dwell in Christ in order that through him he might "reconcile to himself all things, whether on earth or in heaven, making peace by the blood of his cross" (1:20).

The description of his person was leading up to a declaration of his purpose, to reconcile all things to God.

Background of Colossians

In order to appreciate most fully the book of Colossians with its great Christological passages, it is essential that we know something of the background of the city and the insidious heresy that was attempting to make its inroads into the church.

Colossae was one of the cities along the shores of the Lychus river, a tributary of the Meander river, in southwest Asia Minor. In Paul's day it had enjoyed a long and prominent role, being on the main trade route between Syria to the east and the seaports of the Aegean Sea to the west. It was one of a triad of cities in the Lychus Valley within easy walking distance of each other, the other two being Laodicea and Hierapolis. With the passing of time, Laodicea became the political and banking center of the area and Hierapolis became a tourist resort because of its celebrated spa waters with their alleged healing qualities. By comparison, Colossae had declined somewhat in prominence, but was still a well-known and thriving city.

It is of historical interest to note that this section of Asia Minor was once a part of the ancient Hittite Empire, which in many respects rivaled Egypt in its culture and artifacts of an advanced civilization. Subsequently, around 1200 B.C., the region was invaded by the Phrygians and Thracians from central Europe and took the name of Phrygia. Still later it was dominated in turn by the Persians, the Greeks, and the Romans. Today it is a part of Turkey. In Paul's day Colossae was a part of the Roman province of Asia. The city of Ephesus, where Paul had spent some two and a half years in ministry, was approximately one hundred miles to the west.

Because of its changing populations and cultures, the region had become a kind of melting pot, not only of different races but also of diverse cultures and religious beliefs and practices. Here the religions of the east met those from the west. In addition, the so-called "mystery religions" had found their way up from Egypt. Here one might find devotees of Zeus, Apollo, Cybele, Pluto, Isis, Serapis, and other gods and goddesses. The Lychus Valley seems to have provided fertile soil for many different cults, resulting in a medley of beliefs and practices.

One of the Prison Epistles

Colossians is known as one of the prison epistles, the other three being Philippians, Philemon and Ephesians. While some scholars have questioned the authenticity of Paul's authorship of Ephesians, this writer is led to accept either the absolute genuineness of this epistle, or at the very least that it was written by someone who correctly reflects the thought of Paul. In none of these letters does Paul state the place of his imprisonment. What trouble he might have saved future scholars if only he had dropped the name of the city from which he was writing. One thinks first and most naturally of Rome, and for many years this was the generally accepted place, but in more recent years other scholars have contended for Caesarea or Ephesus. There are interesting points raised in favor of one or the other of these. However, all things considered, this writer is inclined to abide with the traditional view of Rome.

The Coming of Epaphras

Epaphras had been serving as the minister of the church in Colossae and also had had a hand in the establishment of the churches at Laodicea and Hierapolis (Col 1:7; 4:12–13). Reading between the lines, he probably had come into contact with Paul in

Ephesus and may have been one of Paul's converts. He was one, among others, who went out from Ephesus in an attempt to extend the gospel to other areas of Asia. With Paul's blessing, he had gone to the Lychus Valley. There he located in Colossae, but also extended his efforts to Laodicea and Hierapolis. With the arrival of the news of Paul's imprisonment, Epaphras felt that he should go to him to be of whatever aid and comfort he might afford. He also went as an emissary of good will from the Colossian Christians, although they had never seen Paul personally (Col 2:1).

Epaphras arrived in Paul's presence not only with his personal greetings and the good wishes of the Colossian Christians, but with some disturbing news as well. He told Paul about some false teachers in Colossae, who designated themselves "philosophers," who were teaching things quite contrary to the gospel as Epaphras had received it from Paul, and were undermining the faith of some. There were many good and devout people who were being misled. Epaphras frankly did not know how to deal with the situation and felt that his word, against the word of the so-called "philosophers," did not carry enough authority. He needed help!

Letter to Colossae

After hearing what Epaphras had to say, and after much prayer, Paul, together with Epaphras, decided that the best course of action would be for Paul to write a letter to the church at Colossae. However, Paul suggested that Epaphras remain with him, which would satisfy the Colossians that he was fulfilling his mission of being of aid to Paul and would allow the letter to do its work, thus removing Epaphras from the center of the fray for the time being. In due course, he would be able to return to Colossae and continue his ministry among them.

The letter would be hand-carried by Tychicus, who was to be also the bearer of another letter written to Philemon, a resident of Colossae. Tychicus would be accompanied by Onesimus, the runaway slave who was being returned to Philemon, "no longer as a slave but more than a slave, as a beloved brother" (Phlm 1:16). About his letter-carrier, Paul writes:

> Tychicus will tell you all about my affairs; he is a beloved brother and faithful minister and fellow servant in the Lord. I have sent him to you for this very purpose, that

you may know how we are and that he may encourage your hearts, and with him Onesimus, the faithful and beloved brother, who is one of yourselves. They will tell you of everything that has taken place here (Col 4:7–9).

So Epaphras remained with Paul, and the letter, carefully worded and with much prayer, was sent on its way to Colossae. In passing, we may note this as another instance of how "God works in mysterious ways his wonders to perform." Had there been no false teachers in Colossae, and had Epaphras not come to Paul with his disturbing news, there would be no book of Colossians.

The Colossian Heresy

A heresy is a perversion of truth. Often it takes the form of a half-truth, which is more dangerous than an out-and-out falsehood. A deliberate lie one may easily detect and refute. But a half-truth is subtle, slippery, and hard to handle. The false teachers at Colossae were full of half-truths.

We have already noted that the Lychus Valley was fertile soil for strange cults, resulting in a medley of beliefs and practices. The heresy with which Paul was dealing is best defined as incipient Gnosticism.

Gnosticism takes its name from the Greek word *gnosis* which means knowledge. The superlative of the word is *epignosis* or super-knowledge, and it was this which the false teachers at Colossae claimed to have and to be able to impart to their devotees. Armed with this super-knowledge of the hidden mysteries of the universe, they claimed to have power to overcome the hostile forces which allegedly inhabited the universe and which controlled the fate of people, working ill against them whenever it pleased them to do so.

Gnosticism was based on a philosophy of dualism, the age-long conflict between good and evil, light and darkness. The Gnostics began their system by asking a seemingly valid question: If God is good, then how do we account for the presence of evil in the world which he created? Their answer was first to make a differentiation between spirit and matter, spirit being good and matter being evil, the two forever locked in conflict. If we allow the premise that evil is inherent in matter, then the conclusion follows that a good God could not have created the world.

The Gnostics followed their premise by speculating that God dwells in highest heaven, in the "realm of light," far removed from the mundane universe. He is related to the universe only indirectly through emanations of himself, in a descending order, spoken of variously as demiurgi, angels, principalities, powers, authorities and other terminologies. The rank and significance of such alleged powers depended upon their distance from the original source, or, otherwise phrased, upon their position in the celestial hierarchy. The farther a power was from the original source, the more it became an admixture of evil with good. The powers of the lowest orders, while possessing some divinity, were said to be predominantly evil and hostile to both God and man. It was one of these lower powers that was responsible for the creation of the world of matter, including man.

Man's Predicament

Man himself, they said, is an admixture of good and evil, possessing within himself a spark of the divine nature as spirit, or soul, which, however, is held in bondage within a material body. Throughout one's earthly lifetime there is a continual conflict between flesh and spirit. At the time of death, the spirit (soul) is at last set free from the body and seeks to rise heavenward toward God who dwells in the "realm of light." But to do so, the soul must pass through the various domains of the malignant powers, which are bent on intercepting the soul and holding it captive. Therefore, it is essential to know the proper formulas, or passwords, that will immobilize the evil powers in the different domains and enable the soul to rise above them. This is where "super-knowledge" comes to the rescue. It follows, therefore, that if people expect to reach the "realm of light," it is imperative that they be initiated into the "hidden mysteries" of the higher powers and that they learn the proper passwords.

However, so they taught, not all are capable of receiving such enlightenment, but only a select few who are "spiritually inclined," who possess spiritual "maturity." As for ordinary people, they will have to manage as best they may, but doubtless will fall prey at some point to the hostile powers.

Collectively, the alleged evil spirits which inhabited the regions above were called *stoicheia*, translated "elemental spirits" (Col 2:8, 20; Gal 4:3, 9). Such spirits were said to inhabit the stars and planets and to control the destinies of persons, working their evil designs upon them whenever it pleased them to do so. (We shall leave this subject for the moment and return to it later in the chapter to explore whether Paul himself believed in such hostile powers and, if so, to what extent.)

Worship of Angels

Paradoxically, some of the higher powers were considered good and were to be worshiped. These were the angels. Since God was thought of as being so far distant and unapproachable, it was considered more feasible, and also an act of humility, to worship angels, who in turn would act as mediators to God (Col 2:18).

Pleroma and the False Teachers

One of the key words in the vocabulary of the so-called "philosophers" was *pleroma*. As used by them, it referred to God's completeness within himself, or his absolute perfection, lacking in nothing. It was inclusive of all his powers, attributes, and graces. It came to be virtually synonymous with the name of God. We shall have more to say presently about how the word came to have this theological meaning.

The Place of Christ in Their System

When Epaphras came to the Lychus Valley with his new gospel of Jesus Christ, the Gnostic "philosophers" were quite willing to hear what he had to say and to absorb the new cult into their already syncretized religious system. Somewhere in their celestial hierarchy they were willing to give a place to Christ. But that he was of a low order was evident in the fact that he wore a "body of flesh," and also in the fact that he was the victim of the principalities and powers, unable to save himself from the cross and the death which they inflicted. (See Paul's refutation in 2:15.) Only a part of the *pleroma* (the fullness of God), therefore, could have resided in him, and a very small part at that.

It followed that any redemption which he offered, while not without some value as a sacrifice for sins, was only partial and insufficient, a mere beginning. There remained the cosmic enemies to be overcome, the very principalities and powers from which he had been unable to deliver himself. Since these powers were manifestly stronger than he, how could he deliver from them? Whereas he offered reconciliation of a sort (*katallaga*), what they really needed was "complete reconciliation" (*apoka-tallaga*) from the evil powers of the universe. (The latter is the intensive form of the word.)

Such a reconciliation, or redemption, was possible, they said, only by possessing "super-knowledge" into the "hidden mysteries" of the universe, together with the proper passwords, and this could be obtained only by "initiation" into the "hidden mysteries."[1]

Paul's Answer to the Heresy

Paul's answer was uncompromising and unequivocal. However, his method of attack was not to call up the tenets of the heresy and then proceed to refute them one by one. Rather, he presents his arguments as positive truths of the gospel. If we may respectfully use the term of holy writ, his refutation forms the "shrewdest" writing in the New Testament. He seizes the catchwords and phrases of the opposition (what E.F. Scott aptly calls their "jargon"), and turns them against them.[2] All of this was not done in an hour or two, we may be sure. This epistle shows signs of very careful thought and composition, as much so, in its own way, as Romans and Galatians.

Paul's answer points to the complete deity of Jesus Christ and the absolute adequacy of the redemption which he offers. The core message of Colossians may be summarized and paraphrased as follows:

> You have been forgiven of your sins and totally redeemed by God's beloved Son, who has qualified us to share in the inheritance of the saints in light. He is the very image of the invisible God. He is sovereign over all creation, the one for whom all things exist, and the one in whom all things cohere. He is the head of the body, the church, as attested by his resurrection from the dead. All the fullness of God was pleased to dwell in him, and through him to reconcile all things to God. This reconciliation has been wrought in the body of his flesh through death, thus bringing universal peace by the blood of his cross.

I say this so that you will not be misled by the so-called philosophers who by empty words and deceit would delude you. At the cross he took the initiative and overcame the principalities and powers. He seized the hammer and took the bond written in ordinances against us, which condemned us, and nailed it to the cross, thus canceling it out (2:14). He disarmed the principalities and powers and led them captive behind his triumphal chariot, triumphing over them in it (the cross). (The picture in Greek in 2:15.)

Do not be deceived by what they tell you about "hidden mysteries" and "higher knowledge." In Christ are all the treasures of wisdom and knowledge hidden; having him you have all! Full and final redemption is offered through him to all persons everywhere. Him we proclaim, that we may present every person mature and complete in him.

So I exhort you, as you received Christ Jesus the Lord, so live in him, rooted and built up in him and established in your faith, just as you were taught, always abounding in thanksgiving.

Whence Paul's Lofty Christology?

We are now ready to consider the question: Whence Paul's lofty Christology? It is not surprising that there have been those who have questioned Paul's views of Christ as being imaginative, speculative, and far removed from the humble man of Galilee who went about doing good, preaching the kingdom of God, and teaching the Fatherhood of God and the brotherhood of men. Questions have been raised about Paul's Christology, beginning with some German scholars during the latter part of the last century in the "back to the historical Jesus" movement, which continued into the twentieth century and in more recent years has been revived in the "new quest for the historical Jesus" writings. The main thesis followed by many of these writers is that if we could just get behind the faith of the church and could free Jesus from the subsequent doctrines and speculations attached to him, underneath all these doctrinaire encrustations we would find a beautiful and attractive man who drew people to him by his personality, his message, and his healings, but who still was basically a simple, though brilliant, Galilean peasant. Some even go so far as to speak of Paul as a "corruptor" of the gospel.

On the surface, such views may sound plausible and even appealing to some. However, they are now largely discredited, essentially for three reasons:

(1) First, in the search for the historical Jesus, it has been found impossible to separate what can be known about Jesus from the things most assuredly believed about him and taught by those in the early church. The historical Jesus and the faith of the church are inextricably interwoven.

(2) Second, if we accept the gospel records as they stand, we find that the faith of the church stems from the very things Jesus believed and taught concerning himself. It is not that the church appended foreign doctrines to him, but that Jesus regarded himself as the unique Son of God.[3] He thought of himself as the messiah, though taking the servant model of Isaiah,[4] not the Davidic king model most current in Jewish expectation.[5]

(3) Third, the Christology of Paul is now seen to be in full accord with the faith of the early church. If Paul's mind moves one step back in his presentation of Jesus as preexistent and the agent in creation, the difference is one of degree, not of principle. Belief in the preexistence of Jesus and his agency in creation were logical inferences from the faith that he was God's Son and eternally one with the Father. This faith was substantiated for the early Christians by the resurrection. They confidently affirmed that Jesus was alive and exalted to God's right hand. Belief in the resurrection was the lens which brought many things regarding the person of Jesus Christ into focus for the early Christians as they now saw in him the fulfillment of the scriptures.

The apostle Paul never saw himself as advocating a gospel other than that which was the legacy of those who were apostles before him. He openly acknowledged his indebtedness to what he had received from them (1 Cor 15:3). The first recorded account of the Lord's supper is given by Paul. He begins the account by saying: "For I received from the Lord what I also delivered to you . . ." (1 Cor 11:23). What he had received of the Lord about the institution of this sacrament came by way of the first apostles.

We know from the book of Acts that Paul was very desirous that his ministry have the approval of the apostles and elders in Jerusalem, and he reported to them repeatedly about his mission to the Gentiles. The authorities in Jerusalem may have had some questions about this, although they agreed in principle, but they never questioned his Christology. This is significant. If Paul had been preaching a different Christ, they would have corrected him.

The faith of those in the early church is clearly defined in Acts. They preached Jesus and the resurrection (2:32; 3:15; 4:2, 33; 10:40; 17:18). They proclaimed him as messiah, Lord, judge, and Son of God (2:36; 7:52; 8:35; 9:20; 10:36, 42). They acknowledged that in him they found forgiveness of sins and salvation (2:38; 4:12; 10:43). They experienced his presence in the breaking of bread and worshiped him with prayers and hymns (1:24; 2:42; 7:59). They credited him for having poured out the Holy Spirit upon them (2:33). To them, God the Father and Jesus Christ were inextricably joined; there was no way of disassociating them. God had come to them in his Son. This was the faith of the early church; this was the faith of Paul. It was a natural step to go from the exalted Christ to the preexistent Christ, eternally one with the Father and the agent of God in creation.

The same faith in Christ's preexistence and his agency in creation is, of course, voiced by other New Testament writers, notably by the fourth evangelist and the writer to the Hebrews (Jn 1:1-2; Heb 1:2-3).

Other Factors in Paul's Christology

In addition to what has been said, there were other factors contributing to Paul's Christology. There were theological concepts and writings current in his day with which he would have been familiar. Some of these were Jewish while others had a Greek flavor. There was also the testimony of his own inner experience of salvation. Consider here four elements which contributed to his faith in Christ and his expression of it.

(1) Concept of the Logos

One of these concepts was the doctrine of the Logos. Some have traced the Logos concept back to Heraclitus who lived some five hundred years before Christ. The Greeks were interested in knowing the origin and nature of the universe and tried to trace it back to a single unifying principle, thus making it a universe. Heraclitus saw the universe as being in a state of constant flux, yet governed by a rational element which he sometimes called Harmony but most frequently called Logos, or Reason. The Logos pervaded the universe as a kind of rational energy, unifying and harmonizing its diverse elements.

The use of the term Logos was, for the most part, by-passed by Plato and Aristotle, but was picked up again by the Stoics, beginning with Zeno in the early part of the third century B.C. It was the Stoics who gave the Logos its prominent place in pre-Christian thought. They, along with other Greek philosophers, emphasized the transcendence of God, though without the sense of dualism which was to characterize later Gnostic thought. This transcendent God, they said, created the world by the Logos. The Logos was the rational principle pervading the universe, bringing order and giving meaning to all things. The Logos was the self-expression of God in his gracious disposition toward the world. The Logos was looked upon as the mediator between God and the created order.

The next step in the progression may be said to be in the writings of Philo, one of the greatest Jewish scholars of his day, a contemporary of Paul, and a resident of Alexandria. In Philo, the best in Greek philosophy merged with the best in Jewish theology. Philo equated the Greek concept of Logos with the Jewish "Word of the Lord." In Jewish thought, the "Word of the Lord" was equivalent to God's outgoing self. It was by his Word that creation came into being. God spoke, and it was so. His Word going forth from his mouth became his acting agent to carry out his will (Gen 1; Pss 33:6; 107:20; 147:15; Is 55:11; Jer 23:29).

Since Logos literally means Word, Philo made a natural conflation of the two. In Philo's thought, the Word (Logos) was God's agent in creation and continues as the mediator between God and all things created. All wisdom and other heavenly graces are mediated to men by the Word. Philo often gives the Word other titles, some of them being First-born Son, Image, Wisdom, and Advocate, and can move from term to term on an equal basis.

Paul would have been quite familiar with the Stoic concept of Logos and the Jewish doctrine of the Word, and also may have been familiar with Philo's thought. In the Colossians' passage, Paul ascribes to Christ all of the properties of the Logos, or Word, but without using either term. In his thought, it is God's "beloved Son" who possesses these attributes and who has wrought these deeds of creation and redemption. However, there is one substantial difference between Philo's thought and Paul's. While Philo's thought of the Logos, or Word, is purely abstract, for Paul

Christ is a real, historical person who by his death and resurrection has brought redemption and reconciliation to men and to the universe, and is the true mediator between God and men.

(2) Concept of Wisdom

There is another approach closely related to the foregoing, namely, the Hebrew concept of Wisdom. A considerable body of Jewish writings had come into being known to us as the Wisdom literature. In some of these writings, Wisdom is personified and is portrayed as being co-eternal with God and God's agent in creation, in much the same vein as the Word, or Logos, described above.[6] One example:

> The Lord created me (Wisdom) at the beginning of his work,
>   the first of acts of old.
> Ages ago I was set up, at the first,
>   before the beginning of the earth.
> When there were no depths I was brought forth,
>   when there were no springs abounding with water.
> Before the mountains had been shaped,
>   before the hills, I was brought forth;
> before he had made the earth with its fields,
>   or the first of the dust of the world.
> When he established the heavens, I was there,
>   when he drew a circle on the face of the deep,
> when he made firm the skies above,
>   when he established the fountains of the deep,
> when he assigned to the sea its limit,
>   so that the waters might not transgress his command,
> when he marked out the foundations of the earth,
>   then I was beside him, like a master workman;
> and I was daily his delight,
>   rejoicing before him always,
> rejoicing in his inhabited world
>   and delighting in the sons of men . . ." (Prv 8:22–31).

The apostle Paul, being the rabbinical scholar that he was, would have been thoroughly familiar with the Wisdom literature and the Wisdom concept. In 1 Corinthians he speaks of Christ as "the power of God and the wisdom of God" (1:24). In making the possible connection between the Wisdom concept and the Colossians' passage, Professor C.H. Dodd writes:

In Colossians 1:15–19, without mentioning the word "wisdom," he (Paul) uses language which can be traced in every point (except the one word "fullness") to Jewish Wisdom theology. According to this, Christ (as "life-giving Spirit") is, so to speak, the thought of God projected from Him, to be the principle by which the world is both created and sustained, and finally brought to the perfection designed by the Creator. . . . This "Wisdom-Christology" made it possible for Paul to give a more adequate account of what was meant by calling Christ the Son of God. He did not begin to be such at His resurrection, or at His baptism, or at His birth. He is a revelation in time of the eternal Wisdom, or thought of God, proceeding from Him, yet eternally one with Him.[7]

(3) Concept of Pleroma (Fullness)

We return to examine the word *pleroma* (fullness), and to trace as best we may how it developed in a theological sense. When Paul used the word in Colossians, it already had a distinct theological connotation which Paul did not feel necessary to explain. Bishop J.B. Lightfoot, in his commentary on Colossians, has a special section on the word *pleroma* in which he says:

It will be evident, I think, from the passages in St. Paul, that the word Pleroma, "fullness, plenitude," must have had a more or less definite theological value when he wrote. . . . The absolute use of the word, "all the Pleroma," would otherwise be unintelligible, for it does not explain itself.[8]

Can we then trace the origins of the use of *pleroma* in a theological sense? I believe that we can. We need to remember that *pleroma* can mean not only "fullness" but "completeness," and therefore "perfection." It came to represent God in his perfection, his possession of all the graces, attributes, and powers associated with deity, lacking in nothing.

We begin with a metaphysical concept which we find in both Hebrew and Greek thought that God is everywhere present. There is no place that is void of his presence. In Jewish theology this was virtually taken for granted. Consider Psalm 139 as one example:

> Whither shall I go from thy Spirit?
>   Or whither shall I flee from thy presence?
> If I ascend to heaven, thou art there!
>   If I make my bed in Sheol, thou art there!
> If I take the wings of the morning
>   and dwell in the uttermost parts of the sea,
> even there thy hand shall lead me,
>   and thy right hand shall hold me (vv. 7–10).[9]

In the New Testament, Paul expresses a similar view of God's omnipresence as, in his speech in Athens, he declares:

> The God who made the world and everything in it, being Lord of heaven and earth, does not live in shrines made by man, nor is he served by human hands, as though he needed anything, since he gives to all men life and breath and everything. . . . He is not far from each of us, for "In him we live and move and have our being" (Acts 17:24–28).[10]

We have seen how in Greek thought likewise, God, while viewed as transcendent, nevertheless filled the universe with his presence as Spirit, Logos, Wisdom, Reason, or Mind. Philo, who bridges the gap between Hebraic and Hellenistic thought, speaks frequently of the omnipresence of God, who fills all things by means of his Spirit, Logos, Wisdom, Providence, or Powers.[11]

The next step in the progression has to do with the metaphysical concept of space and place. Whereas God is everywhere present, and, as it were, contains all things, he himself is not contained. He is full and complete within himself, sufficient unto himself. This came to be a common teaching in Hellenistic thought. For example, Philo writes:

> There is a third signification (of place), in keeping with which God himself is called a place, by reason of his containing all things and being contained by nothing whatever, and being a place for all to flee into, and because he is himself the space which holds him; for he is that which he himself has occupied, and nought encloses him but himself. I, mark you, am not a place but in a place; and each thing likewise that exists; for that which

is contained is different from that which contains it, and the Deity, being contained by nothing, is of necessity Itself Its own place (*De Somniis*, I, xi, 63–64).[12]

W.L. Knox in his book, *St. Paul and the Church of the Gentiles*, summarizes this concept for us:

> It was again a general conception of the age that the whole cosmos was completely "full"; there was no vacuum in it. But the material world was always giving out and taking in; fullness was properly a quality that belonged to God alone" (p. 163).

Thus, *pleroma* came to be used as a term associated with God, signifying his completeness and perfection. He is the one who is full and complete within himself, possessed with all graces and powers, whose presence fills all things. The terms *"pleroma"* and "God" were virtually synonymous.

Within this context it is evident that Paul used the word *pleroma* to apply to both God and his Son, Jesus Christ. He took the word and filled it with Christological significance. Not for a moment would he entertain the suggestion of the false teachers ("philosophers") that Jesus was "a deity of a lower order because he possessed a body of flesh and was overcome on a cross." On the contrary, Jesus in bodily form (2:9) possessed all the *pleroma* (fullness) of God, and on the cross he made the supreme sacrifice for sin. Through him all things, whether on earth or in heaven, have been reconciled to God, peace having been achieved "by the blood of his cross" (1:19–20).

(4) His Personal Salvation Experience

There was one further element that was basic to Paul's high Christology, namely, his personal salvation experience. His Damascus road encounter reversed everything for him. From that moment forward, he knew that Jesus was alive and a vital life force. The resurrection confirmed all the affirmations that the disciples had been making about him as the messiah, the Son of God, and redeemer.

Yet the proof was not by outward sign only. Paul experienced within himself an amazing transformation leading to daily renewal in the Spirit. A sense of the forgiveness of sins, of joy, peace, purpose, and the power of the Holy Spirit, flooded his heart. The mystical presence of Christ became his driving motivation. Sharing mystically in the life of Christ, he died to his old self (2:20; 3:3) and was raised with Christ to newness of life (3:1). His experience with Christ ("in Christ") proved to be in every sense a God-experience. Therefore, nothing that he might say about him was too great. The concepts of Logos, Word, Wisdom, and *pleroma* all applied to him. Indeed, they were but feeble attempts of language to express the inexpressible, for no human terms could do justice to him, define him, or explain him. Perhaps the words of the Nicene Creed of later years would come as close as any to expressing Paul's thought: "Light of Light, Very God of Very God."

The Question about "The Elemental Spirits of the Universe"

As promised earlier, we return to consider the phrase "the elemental spirits (*stoicheia*) of the universe." Four times the term appears in the writings of Paul: Colossians 2:8, 20; Galatians 4:3, 9. In Paul's day there was widespread belief in astrology. Each star or planet was said to have its own spirit inhabiting it. Some of these were good while others were viciously evil, bent on working their malicious wiles on people. The course of a person's life was allegedly determined by the star under whose influence one was born. Every illness, every defect, every mishap was said to be the work of some malevolent spirit. It is difficult for us in a more enlightened age to realize the awful weight which such beliefs imposed, not only on the simple-minded, but upon educated people as well. Those who held such beliefs felt themselves oppressed and helpless in the face of circumstances beyond their control.

The immediate question before us is whether Paul himself believed in the reality of such evil powers inhabiting the stars and planets and holding their fateful grip on persons. There are those who say that Paul was simply "a child of his age" and did so believe. This writer does not agree.

Far from being "a child of his age," he was often at odds with prevailing pagan ideas of his day. For example, at Athens, an intellectual center, he pointed to the many idols and altars of their city only to direct them to the true God "in whom we live and move and have our being" (Acts 17). In like manner in his first letter to the Corinthians he makes a clear distinction between false gods and the one true God:

> For although there may be so-called gods in heaven or on earth—as indeed there are many "gods" and many "lords"—yet for us there is one God, the Father, from whom are all things and for whom we exist, and one Lord, Jesus Christ, through whom are all things and through whom we exist (1 Cor 8:5–6).

The task of interpreting the meaning of *stoicheia* in both Galatians and Colossians is made difficult because of the different ways the word is to be understood, depending on context. Literally it means "things set in a row." It came to be applied particularly to the letters of the alphabet and hence to anything of an elementary or rudimentary nature. Next it was applied to the basic elements which supposedly constituted all things: earth, air, fire, and water. The next step was to apply the term to the sun, moon, stars, and planets, because presumably they were composed of these primordial elements. From here it was a single step to apply the term to the spiritual powers that allegedly inhabited and presided over the stars and planets. We should note also that *cosmos* may be translated as either "world" or "universe."

In the fourth chapter of Galatians where the word occurs twice (vv. 3 and 9), Paul was appealing to the Galatians to stand fast in the freedom which they had received in Christ and not to retrogress to become again slaves to the *stoicheia* of the cosmos. Translators and commentators are about evenly divided as to whether the reference is to "the elemental spirits of the universe" or to "the elemental things of the world." However, if we take the first translation, the fact that within the same paragraph Paul speaks of "beings that by nature are no gods" (v. 8) leads us to believe that Paul himself did not look upon the "elemental spirits" as real entities.

At Colossae the situation was different. The false teachers ("philosophers") apparently had developed already a fairly elaborate hierarchical system of higher powers (very common in later Gnosticism) and were saying that these powers had overcome Christ on the cross. Paul might have taken the course of argument that all of this was nonsense because the alleged elemental spirits were non-entities—"no gods." But this would have called for a discourse in the field of metaphysics where the "philosophers" might have countered that their views were as valid as Paul's, and certainly more widely held. So Paul took another line of approach. He did not argue the existence of the elemental spirits, but only for the supremacy of Christ over them:

> See that no one makes a prey of you by philosophy and empty deceit, according to human tradition, according to the elemental spirits (*stoicheia*) of the universe, and not according to Christ. For in him the whole fullness of deity dwells bodily, and you have come to fullness of life in him, who is the head of all rule and authority (2:8–10, RSV).

It was within this paragraph that Paul also affirmed:

> He disarmed the principalities and powers and made a public spectacle of them, triumphing over them in it (the cross) (2:15).

The second appearance of *stoicheia* in Colossians (v. 20) occurs in the midst of Paul's warning against a false asceticism. Here the translation "the elementary things of the world" would be more appropriate than "the elemental spirits of the universe." The reading would then be:

> Therefore let no one pass judgment on you in questions of food and drink or with regard to a festival or a new moon or a sabbath. These are only a shadow of what is to come; but the substance belongs to Christ. . . . If with Christ you died to the elementary things (*stoicheia*) of the world, why do you live as if you still belonged to the world? Why do you submit to regulations, "Do not handle, Do not taste, Do not touch" (referring to things which all perish as they are used), according to the injunctions and teachings of men? (2:16–22).

At the same time, there are other passages of scripture which lead us to believe that Paul did hold credence in some kind of evil spiritual forces working in antagonism to both God and mankind. He spoke of his thorn in the flesh as "a messenger of Satan" (2 Cor 12:7). It was Satan who hindered his purposed visit to Thessalonica (1 Thes 2:18). Of our struggle against evil, he says:

> For we are not contending against flesh and blood, but
> against the principalities, against the powers, against the
> world rulers of this present darkness, against the spiritual
> hosts of wickedness in the heavenly places (Eph 6:12).

In Romans 7, where he tells of his personal struggles (possibly
his pre-Christian experiences), he confesses to his human weakness, for he always ends up doing the very things he hates, and
fails to do the good that is his purpose. It is as if some evil power
controls him, forcing him to act contrary to his own will. In
Romans 8, however, where he describes life in the Spirit, the
situation is reversed and evil is put to rout. The Spirit-filled life
conquers all. He calls the roll of all real or alleged powers, or
conditions of human experience: death, life, angels, principalities,
powers, things present, things to come, height, depth, and anything else in all creation, and concludes that none of these will be
able to separate us from God's love in Christ Jesus our Lord.
Whatever evil powers there may be are no match for the person
whose life is linked to God.[13]

We are led to this conclusion: that whereas Paul believed in
some form of evil spiritual forces opposed to both God and mankind, there is not sufficient evidence to say that he looked upon
these forces as evil spirits inhabiting the stars and planets and
holding their sway over persons as fate and destiny. While such
beliefs were prevalent in pagan circles, there is no warrant to
conclude that the apostle's view was carried to that extreme.

3

Kenosis—The "Self-Emptying" of Jesus Christ

And therein (in the books of the Platonists) I read, not indeed in these words, but to the same purpose, enforced by many and diverse reasons, that "In the beginning was the Word, and the Word was with God, and the Word was God." . . . But that "the Word was made flesh, and dwelt among us," I read not there. For I traced in those books, said differently and in many ways, that "the Son was in the form of the Father, and thought it not robbery to be equal with God," because naturally he was the Same Substance. But that "he emptied himself, taking the form of a servant, being made in the likeness of men, and found in fashion as a man, humbled himself, and became obedient unto death, even the death of the cross" . . . those books do not contain (*The Confessions of St. Augustine,* Book VII, Chapter IX).

In the last chapter we explored Paul's lofty Christology, especially as reflected in his use of the term *pleroma*, the fullness of God in Christ. We now turn our attention to another great passage of scripture in which Christ is pictured as "emptying himself" of divine prerogatives to take the form of a servant. The entire passage reads as follows:

Have this mind among yourselves, which you have in Christ Jesus, who, though he was in the form of God, did not count equality with God a thing to be grasped, but emptied himself, taking the form of a servant, being born in the likeness of men. And being found in human form he humbled himself and became obedient unto death, even death on a cross. Therefore God has highly exalted

him and bestowed on him the name which is above every
name, that at the name of Jesus every knee should bow,
in heaven and on earth and under the earth, and every
tongue confess that Jesus Christ is Lord, to the glory of
God the Father (Phil 2:5–11).

An Undogmatic Setting

It is to be observed that this great statement about Christ
occurs in a most undogmatic setting. Paul's purpose at the time
was not to write a theological treatise but to cite a supreme example of humility and self-giving.

The epistle to the Philippians was written primarily as a letter
of appreciation to thank his friends for their thoughtful gift to him
while in prison, a gift that warmed his heart. Although he does not
mention the gift as such until chapter four, his appreciation for
the Philippians themselves overflows in chapter one as he speaks
of his high esteem of them and affection for them. He shares with
them information about how he is faring and encourages them to
endure courageously any hardship which they may be called upon
to bear. In chapter two he undertakes to deal with a problem at
Philippi about which doubtless Epaphroditus, their representative, had informed him. The problem, not an uncommon one in
local churches, was that there was friction between some of the
members. Apparently there was some rivalry in leadership, resulting in ill feelings among some. Whether this was related to the
rift between Euodia and Syntyche which he mentions in chapter
four is uncertain.

Any dissension within the body of Christ was always a source
of grief to Paul. So, in chapter two, he begins by making a strong
appeal for Christian unity. Unity does not mean uniformity, but
demands a mutual love and respect for one another and a willingness to put aside one's own personal preferences in favor of the
desires of others. As a supreme model of unselfishness, he cites
the example of Christ who exchanged his heavenly status with
God to take the form of a servant, in the likeness of men. Beyond
this, he humbled himself further in becoming obedient unto
death, even death upon a cross! Self-abnegation knows no limits
beyond this!

The second half of the passage deals with the exaltation of the
servant. He is rewarded by being exalted to God's right hand and
given the name that is above every name, that he might be universally worshiped as "Lord," to the glory of God the Father.

An Early Christian Hymn

Even in the English translation, one cannot avoid being aware of the rhythmical flow of language and balance of clauses in Philippians 2:5–11. Most New Testament scholars now agree that this passage was originally in the form of poetry and that Paul was quoting one of the early Christian hymns. We are especially indebted to the pioneering work of the German scholar, Ernst Lohmeyer, for his careful analysis of this passage,[1] but there have been others as well who have largely confirmed his findings. The following is the arrangement suggested by Lohmeyer. He divides the hymn into six strophes:

> Who being in the form of God
> did not count it something to be grasped
> to be equal with God,
>
> but emptied himself,
> taking the form of a servant,
> being born in the likeness of men.
>
> And being found in human fashion,
> he humbled himself
> and became obedient unto death
>   (even death on a cross).
>
> Therefore God has highly exalted him
> and bestowed on him the name
> which is above all names,
>
> that at the name of Jesus
> every knee should bow
> in heaven and on earth and under the earth,
>
> and every tongue confess
> that Jesus Christ is Lord
> to the glory of God the Father.

The poetic rhythm is even clearer in the Greek. Some think that the Greek was a translation from Aramaic. Something is always lost in poetic rhythm in attempting to translate. Even so, the poetic quality is evident in English. It should be noted that the rhythm is broken in the third strophe by the addition of a fourth line, "even death on a cross," which Lohmeyer has put into parentheses. It is reasoned that as Paul was quoting the hymn and came to this point, he added the phrase, "even death on a cross." In the original hymn, death is presented as the supreme limit of obedience and self-sacrifice, but at this point Paul breaks in to say that death itself was not the ultimate limit; it was death on a cross! By this added phrase, Paul underscores the utter depth of Christ's condescension.

Assuming that Paul was quoting a well-known Christian hymn, it is interesting to think that here we have a reflection of very early Christian tradition, a creed that was held in early Christian circles and was known and sung in at least some of the churches across the empire. The very fact that Paul quotes it to the Philippians suggests that they were familiar with it. It was something which Paul and they had sung together.

Some people may be reluctant to accept the interpretation that the words did not originate with Paul, as though this would somehow subtract from their inspiration. To this writer the reasoning should be just the opposite. It is surely highly significant that this great statement about Christ was a part of the faith of the early Christian community and is quoted by Paul, with approval, as a part of his exhortation to true humility and servanthood.

Relation to the Servant of Deutero-Isaiah

It is generally recognized that there is a close relationship between the hymn in Philippians 2:5–11 and the servant portrayed in Deutero-Isaiah. In other words, the writer of the hymn presents Jesus Christ as the embodiment of the servant in Deutero-Isaiah.

There are a number of servant passages referred to as "servant songs," which are listed for ready reference:

Isaiah 41:8–10
Isaiah 42:1–9, 18–20
Isaiah 49:1–13
Isaiah 50:4–11
Isaiah 52:13–53:12
Isaiah 61:1–3

It is not our purpose here to discuss these "servant songs" in detail, which would make an interesting study in itself but which would carry us afield from our main theme. Rather, our intent is to indicate the correlation between the Philippian hymn and the greatest and best known of the servant songs, Isaiah 52:13–53:12.

In this servant song, the servant of the Lord is misunderstood and rejected by his own people. Yet, in his own person, he bears their griefs and carries their sorrows; he is wounded for their transgressions; he pours out his life as a sin-offering in their behalf; he gives his life of his own volition for them. In long perspective, however, he is able to see the fruit of the travail of his soul and is satisfied. God lifts him up and gives him a position with the great.

In addition to the general theme of this servant song finding its parallel in the Philippian hymn, there are correlations of particular words and phrases. While these are easier to see in the Greek, they are evident also in the English translation. Consider the following:

(1) Isaiah 52:13—"Behold, my *servant* shall prosper . . ."
    Isaiah 53:11—"By his knowledge shall the righteous one, my *servant*, make many to be accounted righteous."
    Philippians 2:7—"He emptied himself, taking the form of a *servant.*"
(2) Isaiah 53:8—"In his *humiliation* justice was denied him." (Septuagint translation. See Acts 8:33.)
    Philippians 2:8—"He *humbled* himself . . ."
(3) Isaiah 53:12—"He poured out his soul *unto death.*"
    Philippians 2:8—"He became obedient *unto death.*"
(4) Isaiah 52:13—"He shall be *exalted* and lifted up and shall be *very high.*"
    Philippians 2:9—"Therefore God has *highly exalted* him and bestowed on him the name that is above every name . . ."

Both the general theme and the specific language of the Philippian hymn correspond to this servant song of Deutero-Isaiah.

It needs to be noted that the Greek has two words for "servant," as follows:

(1) The first is *doulos,* which may be translated as servant, or slave, or bondslave.

(2) The second is *pais,* which carries a double meaning of child (male or female) and servant. Since a child was regarded as

subservient to his or her parents, and obedient to them, he or she might be regarded as a servant, albeit a very dear and special one. Thus *pais* may mean either a young child or a faithful and beloved servant. In translation, one must rely upon the context for the proper meaning.

In the Septuagint translation of Deutero-Isaiah both *doulos* and *pais* are used of the servant, though *pais* is the more frequent.[2] In some of the same passages, both *doulos* and *pais* are used interchangeably, each meaning the servant of the Lord (Hebrew: *ebed Yahweh*).

In the early church, *pais* seems to have been the favorite word when referring to Jesus as servant (Acts 3:13, 26; 4:27, 30). However, contrariwise, in Philippians 2:5–11, the servant is *doulos*, corresponding to the Septuagint translation of Isaiah 53:11.

Three Portraits of the Messiah

The scriptures present not one portrait of the messiah, but three:

(1) *The first is that of the Davidic-king.* By far, this was the most popular and widespread concept among the Jews. David was their national hero. They longed for a messianic successor to right wrongs, to put down enemies, and to establish God's rule from Jerusalem. The following passages will serve as typical samples of this hope:

Behold, a king shall reign in righteousness . . . (Is 32:1).

For to us a child is born,
    to us a son is given. . . .
Of the increase of his government and of peace
    there will be no end,
upon the throne of David, and over his kingdom,
    to establish it, and to uphold it
with justice and with righteousness
    from this time forth and for evermore.
The zeal of the Lord of hosts will do this (Is 9:6–7).

Behold, the days are coming, says the Lord, when I will raise up for David a righteous branch, and he shall reign as king and deal wisely, and shall execute justice and righteousness in the land. In his days Judah will be saved, and Israel will dwell securely. And this is the name by which he will be called: "The Lord is our righteousness" (Jer 23:5–6).

There are many other such passages pointing to the Davidic-king type of messiah.[3]

Closely allied to the Davidic-king concept was the idea of sonship. Psalm 2 was given a messianic import:

> I will tell of the decree of the Lord:
> He said to me, "You are my son,
>   today I have begotten you" (v. 7).

Also, Psalm 89:

> He shall cry to me, "Thou art my Father,
>   my God, and the Rock of my salvation."
> And I will make him the firstborn,
>   the highest of the kings of the earth (vv. 26–27).

(2) *A second messianic concept is that of the apocalyptic Son of Man,* stemming from Daniel's vision:

> I saw in the night visions
> and behold, with the clouds of heaven
>   there came one like a son of man,
> and he came to the Ancient of Days
>   and was presented before him.
> And to him was given dominion
>   and glory and kingdom,
> that all peoples, nations, and languages
>   should serve him;
> his dominion is an everlasting dominion,
>   which shall not pass away,
> and his kingdom one
>   that shall not be destroyed (Dan 7:13–14).[4]

With the passing years and the ever receding hopes of the fulfillment of the Davidic-king messiahship, many Jews were attracted to the Son of Man concept. According to this, at some point in time God himself, through the Son of Man, will forcefully intervene in history, to establish his reign of righteousness.

It is to be observed that in this second concept the Son of Man appears as a heavenly figure, not an earthly one, and that he is commissioned to establish a kingdom that shall not pass away.

(3) *The third portrait of the messiah in scripture is that of the servant of the Lord.* Although the servant of the Lord thesis was written deep into the scroll of Deutero-Isaiah, it was largely ignored by Jewish interpreters, or was reinterpreted to mean something quite different from the natural meaning of the language.[5] The Jewish leaders could not entertain the thought that their messiah should suffer. Such a thing was unthinkable, diametrically opposed to their hopes.

Jesus and the Servant Role

The servant songs, however, made a profound impression on the mind of Jesus. More than any other portions of scripture, they were to define the role he was to fulfill. He saw himself as a true servant of the Lord, wholly obedient to God and wholly compassionate and empathetic to the needs of others. This called for a life of outgoing service in their behalf.

In his first discourse in his home town of Nazareth, when he was invited to read from the scriptures and to make an interpretation, he turned to the scroll of Isaiah and found the place where it is written:

> The Spirit of the Lord is upon me,
> because he has anointed me to preach good news to the
>   poor.
> He has sent me to proclaim release to the captives
> and recovering of sight to the blind,
> to set at liberty those who are oppressed,
> to proclaim the acceptable year of the Lord (Lk 4:18–19,
>   quoting Is 61:1–2).

Closing the scroll and giving it back to the attendant, he sat down for his discourse, as the custom was in teaching, and said: "Today this scripture has been fulfilled in your ears." Jesus found in the servant songs the pattern for his own life.

At a later period, when John the Baptist, languishing in prison, was in a dilemma regarding the role of Jesus, he sent two of his disciples to Jesus with the question: "Are you he who is to come, or shall we look for another?" That day the two emissaries watched Jesus at work. Then he said to them:

> Go and tell John what you have seen and heard: the blind receive their sight, the lame walk, lepers are cleansed, and the deaf hear, the dead are raised up, the poor have good news preached to them. And blessed is he who takes no offense at me (Lk 7:22–23).

He was paraphrasing Isaiah 61:1–2 and 35:5–6. The proof of his messiahship was in his fulfilling the servant role. He hoped that John would understand these prophetic references and find no cause of offense.

It may seem strange that Jesus never used the title "servant of the Lord" with himself as subject. His favorite designation of himself was Son of Man, a title which he used again and again, recorded some eighty times in the gospels. All of the other desirable qualities of messiahship were supposed to be incorporated into that title: his identity with man with all his weaknesses and frailty, as the title itself suggests and was so used by Ezekiel; the royal aspect of the Davidic king, only now in a supernatural sense; and above all the proclamation of "the kingdom of God" associated with the Daniel vision. The one missing element, the servant of the Lord, Jesus was to supply himself, identifying himself with the Son of Man, and the Son of Man with the servant.

The amazing thing in all of this is how Jesus took the best from each messianic concept and combined and recast the desirable elements to come up with a composite messianic ideal that was unique and singularly his own, surely under the Spirit's guidance.

But whereas Jesus never used the title servant of the Lord as subject for himself, he verbalized it. He did not, for example, say: "The servant of the Lord came not to be served but to serve," but rather, "The Son of Man came not to be served but to serve and to give his life a ransom for many" (Mk 10:45). The qualities of the servant were transferred, as it were, to the Son of Man. Likewise, in his predictions of his approaching sufferings and death, a reflection of the servant in Isaiah 52–53, it was the Son of Man who was to endure these things.

> And he began to teach them that the Son of Man must suffer many things, and be rejected by the elders and the

chief priests and the scribes, and be killed, and after
three days rise again (Mk 8:31).

The same prediction of coming events is repeated in similar
language in Mark 9:31 and 10:33–34. To the Jewish leaders, a
suffering Son of Man would have been a contradiction in terms.
They totally rejected the idea. The disciples themselves had difficulty in comprehending and accepting it. Only after the resurrection did they more fully accept it. But it was firm in the mind of
Jesus that he must go to Jerusalem where he would suffer these
things.

In closing this section on the servanthood of Jesus, a quotation from the gospel of Luke will speak for itself:

> A dispute also arose among them, which of them was to
> be regarded as the greatest. And he said to them, "The
> kings of the Gentiles exercise lordship over them; and
> those in authority over them are called benefactors. But
> not so with you; rather let the greatest among you be-
> come as the youngest, and the leader as one who serves.
> For which is the greater, one who sits at table, or one
> who serves? Is it not the one who sits at table? But I am
> among you as one who serves" (Lk 22:24–27).

The Name That Is Above Every Name

The Greek word for Lord is *Kurios.* In Paul's day it had several meanings. It was used first of all as a title of respect and
honor, corresponding to our English *sir,* the German *herr,* and the
French *monsieur.* Sometimes it was used as a recognition of own-
ership, as when a slave addressed his master as Lord. In the course
of time it became a title used of the Roman emperor, and later was
required by him, or by his deputies for him, as an act of loyalty
and worship. It was here that the Christians drew the line, many
of them at the cost of their lives. In pagan circles, it was used as a
title for the heathen gods and goddesses: Serapis, Isis, Asclepius,
Zeus and others. There are some writers who have been quick to
conclude a close correlation between these examples and the title
as used of Jesus by the early church, particularly the analogy to
the gods and goddesses.

However, we do not need to look to extraneous sources when
the chief basis for the title, as used of Jesus, is to be found in the

scriptures themselves. Certainly this should be the first and most logical place to look. In the Old Testament scriptures, one of the names, or titles, used of God was "Lord." It is surely highly significant that the early Christians saw no disparity in taking their most accustomed word for God and using it of Jesus. Not only so, but there were passages from the prophets and the psalms which referred originally to the God of Israel that the disciples now applied in a prophetic sense to Christ.[6] They could justify doing so because they had found God in Christ and through him had experienced redemption. Above all, his Lordship was confirmed to them by the resurrection.

The term Lord has an interesting history. In the Old Testament several names are used of God, but the chief one was *Yahweh* (English, Jehovah; Hebrew, YHWH, without vowel pointings). As *Yahweh*, God had appeared to Moses at the burning bush:

> Then Moses said to God, "If I come to the people of Israel and say to them, 'The God of your fathers has sent me to you,' and they ask me, 'What is his name?' what shall I say to them?" God said to Moses, "I AM WHO I AM." And he said, "Say to the people of Israel, 'I AM has sent me to you' " (Ex 3:13–14).

The name Yahweh is derived from the Hebrew verb "to be," and may be translated "I AM WHO I AM," or "I WILL BE WHO I WILL BE," or simply "I AM." He is the God of being, without beginning, without ending, a name shrouded in mystery.

With the passing of time, when we move into the post-exilic period (ca. 538 B.C. and beyond), the Jewish religion placed such a great emphasis on the holiness and transcendence of God, coupled with a fear of profaning the holy name, that the sacred name of Yahweh was withdrawn from popular usage and substitute words were used to circumvent the pronunciation of the ineffable name. A part of this fear may have stemmed from interpretations placed on Leviticus 24:16 where severe warnings are given against profaning the name of Yahweh.

The most frequent substitute was *Adonai,* which means Lord or Master. Thus, when a reader came upon the name of Yahweh, instead of pronouncing this word he would substitute *Adonai.* Still later, when the Hebrew scriptures were translated into Greek, resulting in the Septuagint, when the translators came upon the word Yahweh, they translated it *Kurios.* Thus, in the Septuagint,

which was widely used by Jews of the dispersion, the most frequently used name for God was *Kurios,* or Lord.

Certainly it was a most noteworthy development that the
early Christians felt that Jesus had so revealed God, had so been
God's instrument of redemption to them, and was so one in nature
with God that they deemed it fitting to appropriate this supreme
title for him. Nor did they consider that they were doing this on
their own, as something which they had contrived. It was God
himself who had conferred on Jesus his own name (Acts 2:36; Phil
2:9). Jesus bore this name "to the glory of God the Father."

The title "Lord," as applied to Jesus, became the church's
earliest creed: *JESUS IS LORD* (Phil 2:11; Rom 10:9; 1 Cor 12:3).
It also became a part of the oath of confession as a person was
initiated as a disciple of Jesus (Rom 10:9). A careful reading of the
New Testament indicates that the title became a very normal and
customary designation of Jesus, frequently occurring alone,
"Lord," and often used in conjunction with the name Jesus, or
Christ, or both together, as "the Lord Jesus Christ."

In a number of places in Acts one cannot tell clearly whether
the author in his use of "Lord" is referring to God the Father, or
to Jesus Christ. For example: "And the Lord added to their number day by day those who were being saved" (Acts 2:47).[7] But
then one gets the impression that it would have made little difference to the author which interpretation was adopted, because
the disciples had come to think of Jesus as so one with the Father
in being, in purpose, and in authority.

Further, the words of Isaiah 45:23, "To me every knee shall
bow, every tongue shall swear," which originally appertained to
God, were now applied to Jesus. It is before him that "every knee
shall bow and every tongue confess that he is Lord." He is to be
universally revered and worshiped. He is exalted and lifted up
and made very high, and is given his portion among the great. His
is the name that is above every name! All of this redounds to the
glory of God the Father.

The Condescension (Kenosis) of Christ

A Brief Theological Survey

The voluntary condescension of Christ spoken of in the Philippian hymn is often referred to in theological circles as his
kenosis, based on the Greek verb meaning "to empty." It has

reference to the verse, "He emptied himself, taking the form of a servant . . ." (Phil 2:7).

The condescension of Christ is stated most specifically in the Philippian hymn and in 2 Corinthians 8:9 where Paul speaks of Christ, though he was rich, becoming poor for our sakes. However, we should recognize that the *kenosis* motif is not confined to any one or two, or more, passages, but is the underlying theme of the New Testament. The very incarnation assumes a condescension.

The writings on the subject of the condescension of Christ (*kenosis*) have been voluminous in the extreme, especially in the latter half of the nineteenth century and extending into the twentieth, stemming primarily from a number of German theologians and followed quickly by other scholars from Switzerland, Sweden, France, Great Britain, and other countries.

In the debate and dialogue, questions were raised, with attempted answers, as to which attributes and powers Christ (the Logos) may have surrendered in the incarnation. Some reasoned that in becoming man, and being truly human, he would have had to renounce all of his divine attributes and prerogatives. Others declared that in becoming man, he renounced nothing, but rather subsumed a human nature in which his divine attributes and powers remained incognito to the general public, except when they were occasionally called forth and used in such measure as necessary to the accomplishment of his mission. Still others attempted to make a distinction between divine attributes necessary to essence (love, holiness, truth) and relative attributes (omnipotence, omniscience and omnipresence) which could be surrendered. The issues were further complicated in trying to deal with the question of how two natures could exist in one person.

The debate on these and like matters seemed to be endless, with no firm conclusions. We shall make no attempt here to detail individual viewpoints, which would be laborious to both the writer and the reader and would require many pages. However, for the person who wishes to pursue the subject further, a helpful bibliography is suggested.[8]

Some have spoken of the *"kenotic theology"* as futile and barren. This writer cannot agree. While the answers may not be finalized, the writings on the unresolved mystery of the incarnation have left us richer for having delved into this paradox.

In all of these writings, coming from competent and dedicated theologians, it is never the deity of Christ that is called into question, but rather how to relate his deity to his humanity.

Of course in every age there have been those who have questioned, or denied, his deity. Some have claimed that he was a man whom his admirers deified. Others have found an answer in a comparison with current myth stories. Still others, on a higher level, have found in Jesus a human being who nevertheless revealed God in a supreme way and therefore might be said to be the moral equivalent of God. But such concepts do not properly belong to the nature of the *"kenotic"* writings we have been discussing, which begin with the recognition of the deity of Christ.

The apostles and other New Testament writers seem not to have attempted to explain the paradox of the incarnation. Their viewpoint was one of juxtaposition. They were too close to the historic life to question his true humanity, yet they had seen in him something that was beyond anything that could be explained in terms of mere human nature. Especially was their view of his divine nature vindicated for them by the resurrection, and we find them repeatedly substantiating their arguments with the phrase, "whom God raised up."[9]

Those writers who say that Christology should begin with the humanity of the man of Galilee rather than with the Trinity are, of course, historically correct, for this is precisely where the disciples began. The doctrine of the Trinity was the outgrowth of the attempt to explain theologically what had been perceived experientially. It was specifically the historical method that the early disciples followed that brought them to the conclusion that Jesus was the Christ and could only be explained in terms of the Godhead.

During the subsequent centuries, any claims which have been put forward for less than this have always been met with a strong and uncompromising rebuttal. A Christ who is merely equated with another human being, however great, be he "John the Baptist, or Elijah, or Jeremiah, or one of the other prophets" (Mt 16:14), is not enough. Professor Donald Baillie writes:

> A toned down Christology is absurd. It must be all or nothing—all or nothing on both the divine and human side. That is the very extreme of paradox.[10]

Jesus Christ was the one "in whom all the fullness of God was pleased to dwell"—"who took the form of a servant, being made in the likeness of men." In the words of the Nicene Creed, it was he who was "Very God of Very God . . . who for us men and for our salvation came down. . . ."

4

The Relevance of the
Paradox to the Incarnation

The heavens decree
All power fulfill itself as soul in thee.
For supreme Spirit subject was to clay,
    And Law from its own servants learned a law,
And Light besought a lamp unto its way,
    And Awe was reigned in awe,
At one small house of Nazareth;
    And Golgotha
Saw Breath to breathlessness resign its breath,
And Life do homage for its crown to death.
    (Francis Thompson, from "Sister Songs")

Two Perspectives

There are two ways to gain appreciation of the height of a skyscraper. The first is to take an elevator to the top and look down from the dizzying height. The other is to stand at the bottom and look up. This is what we do, so to speak, in the two passages from Colossians and Philippians. In Colossians we stand at the height where we see "all the fullness of the Godhead" dwelling in Christ. In Philippians we stand at the very bottom, at the foot of the cross, where we see Christ self-emptied of divine prerogatives and enduring the utmost pain and shame which human depravity can inflict. It is the same Christ seen from different perspectives.

The Idea of Incarnation—
Beyond Human Comprehension

The idea of total divinity and total humanity combined in one person defies human understanding. The Greeks could theorize about God's transcendence, his virtues and his powers, far removed from men, but that he himself could in any way take the form of man and die on a cross was to them "foolishness" (1 Cor 1:18–25). The apostle Paul is quite aware of the dilemma, but says that for those who have experienced his redemptive grace, Christ is "the power of God and the wisdom of God" (1:24). Beyond the rational element, the proof is in the result. Reinhold Niebuhr has well said:

> The idea of eternity entering time is intellectually absurd. This absurdity is proved to the hilt by all the theological dogmas which seek to make it rational. The dogmas which seek to describe the relation of God the Father (the God who does not enter history) and God the Son (the God of history) all insist that the Son is equal to the Father and is yet not equal to Him. In the same way all the doctrines of the two natures of Christ assert that He is not less divine for being human and temporal and not less human and temporal for being fully divine. . . . It is this idea which theology sought to rationalize in the doctrines of the two natures of Christ. It cannot be rationalized and yet it is a true idea.[1]

The Faith of the Early Church

As we have already intimated, the first disciples, including the apostles, probably initially thought of Jesus as a great teacher and prophet, a person who through his prayer life and general demeanor obviously lived close to God and was specially endowed by God to perform mighty works. The fourth evangelist speaks of these mighty works as "signs." The words of Nicodemus probably come close in describing the ground of faith of the early disciples: "Rabbi, we know that you are a teacher come from God; for no one can do these signs that you do, unless God is with him" (Jn 3:2). In addition the early disciples had a personal devotion to Jesus which Nicodemus did not have at that point. It was only gradually that the apostles came to see in Jesus something more than a great teacher, or prophet, or worker of miracles. These categories, while true, were entirely inadequate to describe their experience of him. In his presence, they experienced the very presence of God. In relationship to him, they perceived redemptive grace at work.

It was the resurrection which gave certification to their faith. After the resurrection their testimony to him took on an absolute aspect. His name was conjoined with that of God as the source of forgiveness, joy, peace, and the experience of the Holy Spirit. He became not only the supreme example of faith, but the object of faith. Together with the Father, he became the subject of adoration and worship. We can go even further and say that in him the nature of God was most clearly defined. To paraphrase words of Paul, the light of the knowledge of the glory of God was seen in the face of Jesus Christ (2 Cor 4:6).

The early Christians seem not to have been concerned in reconciling their belief in traditional monotheism with their new faith in Jesus as divine. As for the two natures, human and divine in one person, apparently this did not bother them either. The two natures were held in juxtaposition. They knew that they had witnessed the man, Jesus of Nazareth; no question about that! Neither was there any doubt that they had experienced God in him. While the conflation always allowed for a distinction of persons, Father and Son, they addressed the latter in terms of the divine nature as "the Christ," "Son of God," and "Lord."

Beyond Apostolic Times

When we move beyond apostolic times, Christology passes from its rudimentary stages into something more complex. During the second and third centuries the main theological questions centered in the relationship of Jesus Christ to the Father. For the moment, his relationship to the Holy Spirit was not in question and the subject of the two natures in one person had not surfaced as a theological problem. The major question concerned the relationship of the pre-incarnate Christ, usually spoken of as the Logos, to the Father. Was he equal to the Father or subordinate to him? Was he of the same essence, or subsistence, as the Father? If he was God's Son, his "Only Begotten," was there a time when he was not? Was he subsequent in time to the Father? Learned and conscientious men debated these issues, sometimes with heated animosity, in a spirit that Jesus himself would have disowned.

Decisions at Nicaea

These questions and dissensions led to the calling of the first ecumenical council by the Emperor Constantine in the year 325

A.D. The place of meeting was Nicaea, a city not far from Constantinople. The purpose of the council was to seek some semblance of theological agreement among church leaders and in so doing to help unify the empire. The council was attended by two hundred and twenty bishops who arrived from all parts of the empire. They met for approximately two months. When the council was completed, they had drawn up a formula of faith now universally known as the Nicene Creed. In this creed, Jesus Christ is declared to be ". . . God of God, Light of Light, Very God of Very God; begotten, not made, being of one substance with the Father. . . ."

The Nicene Creed has since been used in most churches as a creedal statement in worship, as a baptismal confession, and often in church courts as a test of orthodoxy. Today it is often found in the front of church hymnals along with the Apostles' Creed. It is the only truly ecumenical creed, accepted by most Christian churches: Greek Orthodox, Roman Catholic, and all major Protestant denominations. The Apostles' Creed, so commonly used in western churches, is acknowledged but rarely used in Greek Orthodox churches, which favor the Nicene Creed.

However, the Nicene Creed did not stop debate. Those who differed with the creed on certain points continued to voice their dissent. In 381 A.D., a second council was called by Emperor Theodosius to meet at Constantinople. While this council took several actions, its basic work was to reaffirm the Creed of Nicaea. No further document was drawn up.

Meanwhile, a number of churches in their use of the Nicene Creed had altered it, partly to correlate it with clauses from the Apostles' Creed, but chiefly to expand upon the role of the Holy Spirit. The original Nicene Creed made only passing reference to the Holy Spirit in a single clause: "We believe . . . in the Holy Spirit."

The Holy Spirit and Christology

Up until the middle of the fourth century, most consideration centered on the relationship of Jesus Christ to the Father as compared to his relationship to the Holy Spirit. In spite of the New Testament emphasis on the Holy Spirit, the church fathers, in their writings on the incarnation, largely ignored the role of the Holy Spirit as they concentrated on the relationship of the Son (Logos) to the Father.

The same omission was demonstrated in the original Nicene Creed, as we have seen, with its single clause devoted to the Holy Spirit. It was not until the meeting of a synod held in Alexandria (362 A.D.) that a doctrine of God emerged in terms of three persons held as a tri-unity; hence the designation: the triune God. At this synod, under the leadership of Athanasius, bishop of Alexandria, the Holy Spirit was declared to be of the same essence as the Father and the Son, though both the Son and the Holy Spirit were considered to be subordinate to the Father.

The delay in the recognition of the affinity of Christ and the Holy Spirit as pertains to Christology seems strange in the light of the witness of the scriptures. In the Old Testament it is stated repeatedly that a mark of the messiah would be that the Spirit of God would rest upon him in a unique and glorious way. In the New Testament, Matthew and Luke relate the conception of the baby Jesus to the Holy Spirit. All four of the gospel writers record the descent of the Holy Spirit upon him at the time of his baptism. John the Baptist compares his own mode of baptism with water, unto repentance, to the baptism that Jesus would administer "with the Holy Spirit and with fire" (Mt 3:11). At the synagogue in Nazareth, Jesus claimed a prophecy from Isaiah as fulfilled in himself: "The Spirit of the Lord is upon me . . ." (Lk 4:18–21).

Some theologians have argued, therefore, that the clue to the incarnation is in a Spirit-filled human being. Whereas the Holy Spirit may reside in each of us in measure, here was a man totally yielded to the will of God and completely filled with the Holy Spirit—a person "in whom the imminence of God dwelt in absolute measure."

On the surface this theory of the incarnation sounds plausible and has its appeal. However, it has its difficulties and has never been generally accepted by the church, for three important reasons. One is that it does not make a clear distinction between the persons, Jesus Christ and the Holy Spirit. Another reason is that it makes the divinity of Jesus relative. Every person experiences the Holy Spirit to some extent. The only difference, then, becomes one of degree. The third difficulty is that this concept borders on "adoptionism," that is, that Jesus was a man whom God chose and adopted to be his Son and the messiah. He was a man who qualified, so to speak, for these positions. For these reasons, this theory of the incarnation, while held by some in every age, has never been the official position of the church.

Chalcedonian Declarations

From about the fourth century to current times, debate in Christology has centered not so much on the relationship of Jesus Christ to the other persons of the Trinity as on the relationship of the divine and human natures in the one person, the incarnate Jesus Christ.

To specifically address these issues, a third ecumenical council was called in 451 A.D., to meet in Chalcedon, near Constantinople. The basic work of this council was to affirm the Nicene Creed in its expanded form, as already widely used in the churches, and to draw up a statement of its own regarding the two natures in Jesus Christ. The text of the Chalcedonian Creed is as follows:

> Therefore following the holy fathers, we all with one consent teach men to confess one and the same Son, our Lord Jesus Christ, the same perfect in Godhead and the same perfect in manhood, truly God and the same truly man, of a rational soul and body, consubstantial with the Father according to the Godhead, and consubstantial with us according to the manhood, like us in all respects, apart from sin; before the ages begotten of the Father according to the Godhead, and in these last days for us and for our salvation of the Virgin Mary, the Mother of God according to his humanity; one and the same Christ, Son, Lord, Only-begotten, to be acknowledged in two natures, without confusion, without mutation, without division, without separation; the distinction of natures being by no means taken away by the union, but rather the property of each nature being preserved and concurring in one person and one subsistence; not parted or divided into two persons, but one and the same Son and Only-begotten, God the Word, the Lord Jesus Christ; according as at first the prophets, then the Lord Jesus Christ himself, taught us concerning him, and as the Creed of the fathers has handed down to us.

It can be seen that in this creed, the full deity and the full humanity are set side by side, conjoined in one person, yet declared to be distinct and separate. Thus the Creed of Chalcedon acknowledges the mystery of the paradox, but does not solve it.

Throughout the ensuing centuries since the Council of Chalcedon, the incarnation has been the subject of much discussion and writings by many theologians. We cannot attempt here an analysis of the different viewpoints. Suffice it to say that after many treatises on the subject, the mystery of the incarnation remains *a mystery*. This is one reason that it remains central to the Christian religion. True religion will always involve mystery. Faith in God does not mean that we have found all of the answers, nor does Christian assurance mean that we have theology tied up in a neat package. There will always be a place for mystery in religion, "for now we see in a mirror dimly."

Two Approaches to Christology

As a general statement it can be said that there are two approaches to Christology, the first known as "Christology from above" and the second known as "Christology from below."

(1) *Christology from above begins with the Godhead.* The place of Christ (the Logos) within the Trinity is already established. With Christology from above, the movement is from God to man. As the story of the historical Jesus begins, his deity is presupposed. Another way of putting it is that Christology begins with the revelation of the scriptures already before us, that we are talking about the Son of God. This is precisely the way the earliest gospel, Mark, begins: "The beginning of the gospel of Jesus Christ, the Son of God." There is no doubt as to who the subject is in the chapters which follow. His divinity is clearly established from the start. In like manner, John, in the prologue to his gospel, introduces at once the Word (Logos) and a few verses later states: "And the Word (Logos) became flesh and dwelt among us" (Jn 1:14). There is no doubt as to whom John is talking about in the remainder of the book.

With Christology from above, the only question, then, becomes *how* such an event as the incarnation could have taken place. In what sense could full divinity and full humanity dwell together in one person? This is the question which was the center of the deliberations at the Council of Chalcedon.

Even when the Christology from above approach is accepted, there are still questions that are left pending. Mark, for example, says nothing about the birth of Jesus and there is no mention of preexistence. Rather, he apparently conceives of his deity as based upon, or confirmed by, his baptism when the Spirit of

God descended upon him. Matthew and Luke carry his deity back to the moment of conception by the Holy Spirit in the womb of Mary. John, writing later, carries his deity back to the eternal Logos.

The apostle Paul does not deal with the mode of the incarnation, but is quite sure that "all the fullness of God" (*pleroma*) dwelt in Jesus Christ. Repeatedly he speaks of him as God's Son. In many places his preexistence is either stated or inferred. From Philippians 2:1–5, Romans 8:3, Galatians 4:4, and 2 Corinthians 8:9, to mention only a few passages, we would conclude that Paul's Christology was one from above. Historically, however, it was rooted in the resurrection and the Damascus road experience.

In like manner, the Christology of the writer to the Hebrews was from above, as we may judge at once from his opening paragraph:

> In many and various ways God spoke of old to our fathers by the prophets; but in these last days he has spoken to us by a Son, whom he appointed the heir of all things, through whom also he created the world. He reflects the glory of God and bears the very stamp of his nature, upholding the universe by his word of power (Heb 1:1–3).

If our take-off point is from the scriptures (with the exception of the book of Acts; see below), it is almost inevitable that Christology be seen "from above." To most theologians, and to Christians in general, this has been the most natural approach.

(2) *Christology from below begins with the historical Jesus.* At the outset of consideration of this approach, it needs to be said that those who take this approach are by no means denying Christ's divinity or the revelation of the scriptures. They may hold equally as high a Christology as those who take the first approach. To refer to the opening analogy of this chapter, it is a matter of whether one views the skyscraper from above or from below.

Christology from below begins with the historical Jesus and moves from there to a recognition of his divinity. Christology from below is concerned first with Jesus and his message, his claims, the effect he had on others, his death, his resurrection, and the proclamation of the early church, all fitted together and leading to the conclusion of his divinity.

Christology from below does not deny the revelation in the scriptures, but goes behind the scriptures to see how they evolved from the faith of the early Christians, under the guidance of the Holy Spirit. As we have seen, the New Testament writers themselves take different approaches to Christology, all assuredly affirming the divinity of Jesus, but not all in agreement as to how this came about.

Those who approach Christology from below are quick to point out that this was precisely the historical process followed in the early church. The first disciples did not start out with a full-blown concept of Jesus' deity. They first became followers of the man, Jesus of Nazareth, a person highly attractive to them by his character, his personality, and his teachings. Even the twelve apostles did not fully realize who he was. Not until the retreat at Caesarea Philippi when Jesus pinned them down with his question "But who do you say that I am?" did they come through with the confession of him as messiah: "You are the Christ" (Mk 8:29; cf. Mt 16:16; Lk 9:20). So, his labors with them had not been in vain! At least they recognized who he was to this extent. This was after three years of close association and shortly before his fatal last journey to Jerusalem.

Yet, even so, their faith did not reach full maturity until after the resurrection. It was the resurrection event that illuminated their minds as to who he really was. The resurrection was like a lens which brought into focus many things which previously had been hidden or only dimly seen. The gospel records tell us repeatedly of things which Jesus told them, "but they understood them not." Then, like the pieces of a jigsaw puzzle when put together, the sayings and events moved into place and the picture of Jesus became clear: this was none other than the Christ, the Son of God, whose death on the cross had wrought atonement for sins, according to the scriptures, and whose resurrection certified him as the anointed one of God. Many passages of the scriptures took on new meaning as they pointed to Jesus as the fulfillment of prophecy.

Mention was made above that most New Testament books take the approach of Christology from above. The one exception is the book of Acts which records the history of the early church. In Acts, Christology is presented as beginning with the historical Jesus of Nazareth. This may have been the most logical course since the apostles and other witnesses were bearing testimony concerning a person whom many of their hearers had seen, heard, and known. Consider the testimony of Peter as we have it in three of his speeches recorded in Acts. At Pentecost, he said:

> Men of Israel, hear these words: Jesus of Nazareth, a man attested to you by God with mighty works and wonders and signs which God did through him in your midst . . . you crucified and killed by the hands of lawless men. But God raised him up, having loosed the pangs of death, because it was not possible for him to be held by it. . . . This Jesus God raised up, and of that we all are witnesses. . . . Let all the house of Israel therefore know assuredly that God has made him both Lord and Christ, this Jesus whom you crucified (Acts 2).

In the temple, after the healing of the lame man, Peter addressed the people:

> Men of Israel, why do you wonder at this, or stare at us, as though by our own power or piety we had made him walk? The God of Abraham and of Isaac and of Jacob, the God of our fathers, glorified his servant Jesus, whom you delivered up and denied in the presence of Pilate, when he had decided to release him. But you denied the Holy and Righteous One, and asked for a murderer to be granted to you, and killed the Author of life, whom God raised from the dead. To this we are witnesses (Acts 3).

In addressing the people gathered in the home of Cornelius the centurion, Peter said:

> Truly I perceive that God shows no partiality. . . . You know the word which he sent to Israel, preaching good news of peace by Jesus Christ (he is Lord of all), the word which was proclaimed throughout all Judea, beginning from Galilee after the baptism which John preached: how God anointed Jesus of Nazareth with the Holy Spirit and with power; how he went about doing good and healing all that were oppressed by the devil, for God was with him. And we are witnesses to all that he did both in the country of the Jews and in Jerusalem. They put him to death by hanging him on a tree; but God raised him on the third day and made him manifest . . . (Acts 10).

Professor C.H. Dodd in his book *The Apostolic Preaching and Its Developments* makes the point that the speeches, or sermons, recorded in Acts are not to be understood as verbatim reports, but as typical of the messages that the apostles brought. He is doubtless correct in this. If the sermons by Peter serve as examples, we see that the apostolic preaching began with Jesus of Nazareth and moved on from there.

Pannenberg's View

One of the noted theologians of our time is the eminent German scholar, Wolfhart Pannenberg. In his comprehensive and knowledgeable book on the incarnation, *Jesus, God and Man,* he rejects the approach to Christology from above, in favor of the historical record in the man Jesus. He writes:

> A Christology from above presupposes the divinity of Jesus. The most important task of Christology is, however, precisely to present the reasons for the confession of Jesus' divinity. Instead of presupposing it, we must first inquire about how Jesus' appearance in history led to the recognition of his divinity.[2]

Pannenberg finds Christ's true unity with God corroborated and finalized in his resurrection. He therefore reasons that Christology should be read neither vertically from above, nor on a linear plane forward, but retroactively from the resurrection event, for it was this that made Christ's unity with God evident and unmistakable to the disciples. His divinity, or "unity with God," as Pannenberg calls it, is verified by the resurrection.[3] At the same time he recognizes the reasons for the development of Christology from above in the faith of the church, with due appreciation of its value.

The Need for Mutual Respect

The differences between these two types of interpretation (Christology from above and Christology from below) should not be overemphasized. The unity is greater than the differences, and both arrive at the same point of the Pauline affirmation: "God was in Christ reconciling the world to himself" (2 Cor 5:19). The fact that both types of interpretation have persisted through the centuries should teach the advocates of each mutual respect and humility. Victor Weisskoff, one of the world's most renowned physicists, has well said: "There are two kinds of truth: the one sees in the opposite something that is wrong and is to be rejected. The other sees in the opposite something that may also contain truth and has something to teach us."[4]

Two Analogies

While working on this chapter, I took a walk at twilight in the glow of a beautiful sunset. The clouds in the western sky were ablaze with color. How do we explain a beautiful sunset? Certainly the origin of it must be the sun (in the celestial sphere). There would be no sight at all without the sun. But it was not the sun alone. There was a reflection of the sunlight from the water vapor and dust particles in the atmosphere (the terrestrial sphere). In addition, there had to be eyes to see and minds to appreciate, God-given endowments. A beautiful sunset is a combination of all of these elements.

Consider another analogy, a common tree. Did I say common? Joyce Kilmer would never have agreed to that! He looked upon a tree as a thing of symmetry and beauty. Certainly a tree might be said to be of the earth, earthy, rooted and grounded in the soil. By a strange process called osmosis it draws from the earth water and chemicals and sends them upward along certain channels to all of its branches. There, by a mysterious process known as photosynthesis, the leaves do a manufacturing job. They capture the energy from the sunlight and combine it with the carbon dioxide taken from the atmosphere and with the water and chemicals taken from the earth and transform them into carbohydrates, which are then sent as food along other channels throughout the tree. A tree is somehow the product of a combination of things terrestrial and celestial.

All analogies are imperfect and break down at some point. In these cases before us, we have dealt with things in the realm of nature rather than Spirit. Yet the analogies can be helpful.

The Mystery Appropriated

While the paradox involved in the incarnation will remain a mystery, this fact should not be permitted to debar us from a full appreciation of it and appropriation of its effects. The incarnation is not just a theory to speculate about and debate in halls of learning. Jesus Christ was an historical person who has come to us where we are, and in his coming has shown us who God is and the meaning of redemptive grace. He is not a person whom one may accept or reject and be none the better or worse for the decision. For in his presence "the kingdom of God has drawn nigh" (Lk 10:11). Just as we may appreciate the beautiful sunset and the symmetry and beauty of a tree without understanding all of the scientific aspects of either, so we may appreciate the wondrous revelation of God in Jesus Christ and appropriate the grace which he brings. The incarnation should never end as a problem to be resolved, but as the prime occasion for thanksgiving and rejoicing.

Fulfillment Through Self-Giving

While the fullness of God in Christ (pleroma) and his self-emptying (kenosis) are seen as contrasts, there is another sense in which they may be viewed as complementary and interacting. His self-giving was the natural result of who he was as *divine Love,* a love that naturally and inevitably expressed itself in outgoing concern for others, even for the most depraved and despicable specimens of mankind. "But God shows his love for us in that while we were yet sinners, Christ died for us" (Rom 5:8).

But in that very giving of self, there was a fulfillment of purpose and a verification of self, hence a sense of achievement and self-fulfillment. The best commentary on this principle is the statement by Jesus himself:

> For whoever would save his life will lose it; and whoever loses his life for my sake and the gospel's will save it (Mk 8:35).

Those words find their prime example in the one who spoke them.

The crucifixion of Jesus Christ, therefore, was his finest moment. His deepest humiliation was his fulfillment.[5] In line with this, the fourth gospel presents his crucifixion as his glorification. Two passages in particular come to mind:

> The hour has come for the Son of Man to be glorified. Truly, truly, I say to you, unless a grain of wheat falls into the earth and dies, it remains alone; but if it dies, it bears much fruit (Jn 12:23–24).

> When he (Judas) had gone out, Jesus said, "Now is the
> Son of Man glorified, and in him God is glorified" (Jn
> 13:31).

His glorification was not simply to follow his humiliation; his hour
of humiliation was his glory! Certainly a very perceptive thought!
Archbishop William Temple comments:

> What we see is not any mere parable of the life of God,
> not an interval of humiliation between two eternities of
> glory. It is the divine glory itself. As we watch that
> human Life we do not say: "Ah—but soon he will return
> to the painless joy of the glory which was his and will be
> his again!" As we watch that Life and, above all, that
> Death, we say, "We behold his glory."[6]

The thought of the apostle Paul is very close to this as he
speaks of the crucifixion, the cross, and the glory:

> But we preach Christ crucified, a stumbling-block to
> Jews and folly to Gentiles, but to those who are called,
> both Jews and Greeks, Christ the power of God and the
> wisdom of God (1 Cor 1:23–24).

> But far be it from me to glory except in the cross of our
> Lord Jesus Christ . . . (Gal 6:14).

The cross, the emblem of disgrace to the world, was the symbol of
grace, power, and glory to the Christian. It remains the chief
symbol of the Christian religion today and deserves this place
of honor.

At the same time, the New Testament writers also speak of
the glorification of Christ following his humiliation, the most notable instance being the Philippians' passage of our consideration:

> Therefore God has highly exalted him and bestowed on
> him the name which is above every name . . . (Phil 2:9).[7]

However, this glorification was but the outward recognition and
acclamation, so to speak, of the glory which he had already won
on the cross.

5

The Relevance of the Paradox to the Atonement

So, the All-Great were the All-Loving too—
So, through the thunder comes a human voice
Saying, "O heart I made, a heart beats here!
Face, my hands fashioned, see it in myself!
Thou hast no power nor mayst conceive of mine,
But love I gave thee, with myself to love,
And thou must love me who have died for thee!"
(Robert Browning, from "An Epistle")

As we come now to consider the atonement, we enter into the holy of holies of the Christian faith. Here, deep calls unto deep. Here, "Thoughts that do lie too deep for tears"[1] grip us. In contemplating the atonement, one's most fitting response is first a hushed silence.

But after the hushed silence, of whatever length, it is also fitting that we step back from the scene and try to understand as best we may this greatest and mightiest act of God's love.

Atone comes from the Middle English word *atonen,* meaning to be "at-one"—in harmony, reconciled. Atonement, therefore, is the state of being reconciled, but in common usage it refers most frequently to the means by which the reconciliation has taken place. It is best understood broadly to include both the means and the state of reconciliation.

The concepts of *pleroma* (fullness) and *kenosis* (self-emptying) throw light on the meaning of the atonement. The first refers to the *person* who has wrought atonement and the second to the *process* by which atonement came. The two concepts mutually involve each other. The first makes the sacrifice of the atonement absolute in nature and the second brings the sacrifice down to our level where it is offered from within humanity Godward,

83

corresponding to our deepest needs, thus effecting our redemption.

Christology and Soteriology

Soteriology is a term used by theologians to refer to the saving work of Christ. It includes all aspects of what we mean by
"being saved," or "redeemed."

There are those who argue, rather convincingly, that Christology (our view of Christ) stems from soteriology (our saving
experience through Christ). Certainly something is to be said for
this. One thinks of Melanchthon's famous statement: "Who Jesus
Christ is becomes known in his saving action."[2] In his chapter
entitled "Christology and Soteriology," Wolfhart Pannenberg
writes:

> The divinity of Jesus and his freeing and redeeming sig-
> nificance for us are related in the closest possible
> way. . . . Nevertheless, the divinity of Jesus does not
> consist in his saving significance for us. Divinity and sav-
> ing significance are interrelated as distinct things. The
> divinity of Jesus remains the *presupposition* for his saving
> significance for us and, conversely, the saving signifi-
> cance of his divinity is the reason why we take *interest* in
> the question of his divinity.[3]

It may be said that Paul's Christology was rooted primarily in
his own experience of redemption, especially his encounter on
the Damascus road. The same principle holds true for any Christian. The printed page and the proclaimed gospel may seem as so
many "idle tales" until the word takes hold of a person and one
experiences in his or her own life the meaning of redemption. The
experience itself is necessary for a true estimate of Christ. It is a
fallacy to assume that one can stand aloof as an unbiased spectator
and arrive at the true facts of his nature. That is one reason why
the "back to the historical Jesus" movement could not succeed; it
was based on the assumption that if only we might divorce ourselves from faith long enough to see him in an unbiased manner,
we would find a quite simple Galilean teacher. But faith itself is a
quite necessary element in the discovery.

It is a well-known fact that the same historical events may call
forth different responses, depending on the element of faith or

the absence of it. The same historical Jesus was hailed by some as the messiah, and denounced by others as an impostor. To Paul, the cross as historical objective fact at one point in his life was a stumbling-block, but later, after his conversion, it became his chief cause for glorying. His faith-experience made the difference. We conclude that Christology and soteriology are interwoven and in experience cannot be separated.

Historical Background of "Atonement"

At this point it is important that we look at the historical background of the concept of atonement. Beyond this, it is essential that we know, insofar as is possible, what was in the mind of Jesus regarding his impending death. Then we shall examine how his death was interpreted in the early church, particularly as seen in the writings of Paul.

Religious Rites in Antiquity

As far back as we can trace religious history, the people of various civilizations and cultures were offering religious rites, including blood sacrifices, to their deity. The question confronts us: Why was there a concept of atonement in the first place?

In answering this question, we begin with the fact that innate to human nature is belief in some form of deity. Written into man's constitution is an intuitive sense that beyond one's self and the material order of things, there is a supreme being. Yet the evidence is not such as to be incontestable or all-compelling. Belief in God is not self-evident. In every age there have been those who have denied the existence of God. Nevertheless, taken on balance, whether it be in primitive societies or in the most advanced civilizations, people have worshiped some form of deity.

Coincident with this belief in a deity is the conviction that the deity makes certain religious and ethical requirements of us. In primitive societies, these requirements may often take the form of taboos. In more enlightened cultures, the ethical requirements may rise to the level of the golden rule. We live in a moral universe in which certain ethical demands are placed upon us. Man is possessed of a conscience which delineates for him the difference between right and wrong and which calls him to account for his response. The consciences of different people may vary widely according to culture, training and enlightenment. However, all persons are born with some innate sense of right and wrong. The apostle Paul was speaking to this when he cited the case of the Gentiles who were born outside the Mosaic law, yet with the law of God written on their hearts:

> When Gentiles who have not the law do by nature what the law requires, they are a law to themselves, even though they have not the law. They show that what the law requires is written on their hearts, while their conscience also bears witness and their conflicting thoughts accuse or perhaps excuse them (Rom 2:14–15).

When man acts contrary to conscience, there is a sense of failure and guilt. Man is responsible for his actions to three parties: to himself, to his fellow human beings whom he may have hurt or offended, and primarily and ultimately to God. Thus David, in his great confessional prayer, says: "Against thee, thee only, have I sinned, and done that which is evil in thy sight" (Ps 51). In point of fact, he had sinned against his own conscience and against Uriah and Bathsheba (2 Sam 11–12), but fundamentally he regarded his offense as against God.

Failure to conform to the ethical standards of God, as written upon the conscience, produces a sense of guilt and alienation from God. It is as though a barrier were erected separating the offender from God, or as though a yawning chasm develops between man and God. In the mind of the sinner, God becomes the accuser and in a sense an enemy. While this may be poor Christian theology, it is characteristic primitive theology.

How is the alienation to be overcome and reconciliation effected? Since man is the offender, it stands to reason that he should be the one to attempt to make amends. In primitive societies the offender felt that he must somehow appease the disfavor of the deity.

(1) *One answer was to bring a gift.* This was usually in the nature of the fruit or grain of the field. Customarily the gift was brought to the place of worship and received by the priest, or representative, of the cult. This method has sometimes been called bargaining. The offender brings an acceptable gift which is offered to the deity, and the offense is annulled.

(2) *A more frequent answer, dating to very remote times, was to make a blood sacrifice.* Usually this was an offering of some domestic animal—a lamb, a goat, a heifer, a bull, a pigeon, a dove,

or some other animal. The grounds for the blood sacrifice lay in the fact that the life of the offender was forfeit to the deity. But since human life was regarded as dear, the life of an animal was offered instead. The life of the offender was represented in the life of the animal that was sacrificed. It was an ancient belief that the life of all animals, including man, was in the blood (Gen 9:4). With the sacrifice, the deity was supposed to be propitiated and the offense canceled.

Offerings and Sacrifices within Judaism

It is, of course, to the offerings and sacrifices of Israel that we must look for the clearest example and type of what, for Christians, was to be the supreme and ultimate sacrifice. The offerings and sacrifices within Judaism comprised an extensive and elaborate system. There were offerings and sacrifices for many different occasions, whether celebrations or for exigencies such as the cleansing of a leper, or the cleansing of the mother after childbirth, or the cleansing of a person after contact with a corpse. Details of laws and procedures are set forth primarily in Exodus, Leviticus, and Numbers, but are referred to in many books.

The sacrificial rites within Judaism did not take place in a vacuum, but find parallels in other nations and cultures dating back into antiquity. At the same time, we like to think (and there is evidence to support the view) that within Judaism the making of offerings and sacrifices had risen above the concept of propitiation, and these were thought of rather as a means of annulling sin and guilt, which is expiation. There is a vast difference between propitiation and expiation. With propitiation, one is dealing with an offended and angry deity. By means of an offering or blood sacrifice, the offrant seeks to change the mind and mood of the deity from hostility to friendliness. With expiation, one is dealing with the offense of the offender. By following the procedure that has been prescribed by God himself in behalf of the offender, sin and guilt are covered, or blotted out, and the person is once more at harmony with himself, as having met the requirements, and with God. Penitence and self-giving are presupposed in the sacrifice. If the offense involved injury to the person or property of another, then restitution was to be made insofar as possible.

Regarding the distinction between propitiation and expiation within Israel, Professor Raymond Abba of the Department of Divinity, University of Wales, says:

The idea of propitiation is not prominent in the Old Testament. The word as a religious term expresses pagan conceptions of appeasing the Deity and is inappropriate to the religion of Israel. . . . In general, at least, Old Testament sacrifices are not propitiatory but expiatory. God is frequently the subject, but never the object, of expiating (i.e. "covering" or "erasing") man's sin, but never in the sense of man's propitiating God. This is in line with the prophetic teaching that God's favor cannot be bought.[4]

Differences of Interpretation

As might be expected, within Judaism there was some degree of fluidity in the observances of the sacrifices, and some changes and adaptations took place from time to time. There were also some differences of opinions as to what actually took place in the presentation of the offerings and sacrifices. Some took a very literalistic approach, saying that the offerings and sacrifices did precisely what was defined in the law. Others found a symbolic meaning in them, feeling that the effect took place in the life of the offrant. For the literalist, the offering or sacrifice tended to be mechanical and staid; the offrant did certain things as prescribed and these acts covered or erased his guilt from the sight of God. For the person who found a symbolic meaning in the rites, worship tended to be on a higher plane. The rites were offered with personal piety and genuine devotion to God such as we find expressed in many of the psalms. The offering of a sacrifice became the occasion for personal prayer and fellowship with God. For example:

> I will offer in his tent
>   sacrifices with shouts of joy;
> I will sing and make melody to the Lord.
> Hear, O Lord, when I cry aloud,
>   be gracious to me and answer me!
> Thou hast said, "Seek ye my face."
>   My heart says to thee,
> "Thy face, Lord, do I seek."
>   Hide not thy face from me (Ps 27:6–8).

The observance of sacrificial rites and devotional prayer life were not looked upon as in conflict, but existed side by side. One might say that the sacrificial rite acted as a trellis upon which prayer life and devotion to God grew.

Types of Offerings and Sacrifices

There were many different offerings and sacrifices, and various authors have used different methods in classifying them. It may be an over-simplification, but it seems to me that they fall into three major categories:

(1) There were the offerings brought as thank offerings, also referred to as peace offerings. Here, the offrant, out of gratitude for blessings received, brought some tangible gift for God, which he normally placed in the hands of a priest. The gift might be of the fruit of the field, or a lamb from the flock, or something else of a tangible nature.

(2) Other offerings were brought in a similar fashion, but with the purpose in mind of making some earnest request of God, not in the sense of buying God's favor, but only to emphasize one's devotion to God as the request was made. An example of this would be the request of Elkanah and Hannah for a son (1 Sam 1).

(3) Most offerings and sacrifices had to do with moral cleansing and the removal of sin and guilt. The usual term for this was "covering" or "blotting out." The customary method was to make a blood sacrifice. In the time of the patriarchs and later, the sacrifice might have been performed personally as the offrant built his own altar and made his sacrifice. With the development of the priestly caste, the usual procedure was to make the sacrifice with the aid of a priest.

Whereas some sacrifices were on an individual basis, other sacrifices were corporate in purpose in behalf of the nation as a whole. In our day, we tend to stress the individual's relationship to God, but in Judaism great emphasis was placed on corporate penitence and corporate redemption. Individual sin and guilt were seen against the larger backdrop of the sin and guilt of the nation.

The supreme example of this was the annual observance of the Day of Atonement. On this significant day the high priest laid aside his priestly garments and ornaments and dressed in a simple white linen robe. He first offered a sacrifice of a bullock for the cleansing of himself, the priesthood, and the sanctuary. With a censer of live coals from the altar, he entered the holy of holies and burned incense before the mercy seat, the symbol of the presence of the Lord. He also sprinkled blood on the mercy seat and floor surrounding it, with a ritual of seven times. This completed the atonement for himself, the priesthood, and the sanctuary.

Two goats were furnished in behalf of the nation. Lots were cast to determine which goat was to be sacrificed and which was to be sent away into the wilderness. The one was then slain and its blood taken into the holy of holies and sprinkled on and around the mercy seat in a similar fashion as described above, but this time in behalf of the nation. Upon the head of the live goat, the high priest laid his hands as he made confession in behalf of the sins of the nation. The goat, symbolically laden with the people's guilt, was then led away and turned loose to roam the wilderness (Lev 16; 23:26–32; Num 29:7–11).

The Sin Offering and Guilt Offering

Within the sacrificial system of Judaism, it is important to give special attention to two sacrifices designated as the sin offering and the guilt offering. On the surface they may sound the same, but to the Jews they were different. Both, however, were expiatory in nature and the rites were similar.

(1) *The sin offering (Hebrew: hattah)* had to do primarily with ceremonial offenses and festival occasions: unwitting sins; touching an unclean object; purification after childbirth; purification of a leper; the consecration of priests; and the festivals of New Moon, Passover, and Pentecost.

(2) *The guilt offering (Hebrew: asham)*, also known as the trespass offering, had to do primarily with offenses against the person or property of others. It involved restitution when possible, plus a penalty-fine of one-fifth the property value. If restitution was not possible to the offended party or his relatives, then the restitution became payable to the priest (Lev 5:16; 6:5; Num 5:7–8).

The sin offering and the guilt offering were similar in many respects and the procedures were almost identical. The two types of sacrifices, though theoretically separate, are difficult to distinguish (e.g. Lev 5:1–13). The main thing to keep in mind is that they were expiatory in nature and were regarded as ordinances prescribed by God for man's benefit for the removal of sin and guilt.[5]

Blood Sacrifices and the Modern Mind

To the modern mind, the idea of blood sacrifices may seem primitive and repulsive. In our more enlightened age, it would seem obvious that God cannot be pleased with the sacrifice of an animal, and to think that he might be borders on heathen superstition. As a matter of fact, the writer to the Hebrews states it plainly: "For it is impossible that the blood of bulls and goats should take away sins" (10:4).

We no longer worship in this way, nor do the Jews, and it is difficult for us to perceive what the sacrificial system meant to those who practiced it. However, with our more enlightened perspective, one must be careful "not to throw out the baby with the bath." All religions are full of symbolism, and it is in the symbolism that one must seek the deeper meaning of the outward acts. The outward acts in themselves are nothing apart from what they are understood to signify. By way of analogy, the same may be said of the Christian's partaking of bread and wine in the sacrament of the eucharist.

Significance of the Expiatory Sacrifices

To grasp the significance of the expiatory sacrifices, let us follow the steps of the procedures, keeping in mind the symbolism behind the outward acts.

(1) First, the offrant, conscious of his sin and guilt, approached the place of worship bringing with him an offering, usually a live animal from his flock. This he presented to the priest, his representative before God.

(2) In the ceremony proper, the offrant laid his hands upon the head of the animal, signifying that his own life was now identified with the victim. The premise behind this act was that, because of sin, the sinner's life was forfeit to God. But rather than his own life being actually sacrificed, the animal's life was offered instead, albeit not as a substitute per se, for the offrant's life was represented symbolically in the sacrificial animal.

(3) The animal was then slain by the offrant as a symbolic act of self-giving to God. The basis for this, as previously noted, was that the life was considered to be in the blood. "The blood is the life" (Lev 17:14; Dt 12:23). "It is the blood that makes atonement, by reason of the life" (Lev 17:11). In later years it was the priest who actually slew the animal, but the symbolism remained the same.

(4) The priest then sprinkled some of the blood on the altar, representing God. In some cases some of the blood was sprinkled before the veil of the sanctuary (Lev 4:6). In some specified cases blood was applied to the offrant (Lev 8:23–24; 14:25). The remainder of the blood was poured out at the base of the altar.

(5) Finally, the body of the slain animal was consumed on the altar of burnt sacrifice, representing the final and complete self-offering of the offrant to God. "And the priest shall burn it upon the altar for a pleasing odor to the Lord; and the priest shall make atonement for him, and he shall be forgiven" (Lev 4:31).

The Old Testament sacrificial system, seemingly so crude in many respects, yet had symbolic roots that ran deep. One must remember that it was regarded as a method laid down by God himself on behalf of his people for the removal of their sin and guilt. In Judaism it was looked upon as an ordinance of forgiveness and redemption, a veritable means of grace.

The Prophets and the Sacrificial System

We are familiar with the strong denunciations of the sacrificial system by the prophets (e.g. Is 1:10–31).[6] In scathing language they denounced those who brought their sacrifices to the altar while at the same time they practiced oppression and injustice toward their fellow men.

It is an unresolved question whether the prophets were advocating abolition of the sacrificial system or were simply seeking to reform it. At the very least, they were denouncing the empty sham of people's offering pious sacrifices to God while at the same time perpetrating oppression and injustice upon their fellow men. Such a situation was intolerable in the eyes of the prophets and in the sight of God for whom they spoke.

While we cannot be absolutely sure whether the prophets were calling for the abolition of the sacrificial system or only for its reform, we do know the course of history. The sacrificial system continued not only to exist but to flourish. Especially was this true following the exile, as we see from the writings of Ezra, Nehemiah and others. Doubtless the injustices, such as the prophets had denounced, could be found as well. However, for the population as a whole, the sacrifices were dutifully offered as prescribed in the law. As noted previously, in the eyes of most pious Jews there was no inconsistency in the observance of the sacrificial rites and personal devotion to God. There were many devout people, of whom Zechariah and Elizabeth would be typical, who offered their sacrifices and who were "righteous before God, walking in all the commandments and ordinances of the Lord blameless" (Lk 1:6).

The New Testament and the Mind of Christ

Turning now to the New Testament, the most important question confronting us is: What must have been the mind of Christ as he approached his death? What were his own thoughts regarding his passion?

The New Testament theology of the atonement cannot be said to have been simply an explanation of the death of Christ developed after the fact by the early Christians. Such an explanation imposed upon his death, giving a purpose for it, would doubtless have helped to soften the blow for them and given some rationale for the cruel fate that had befallen their leader. But there is no hint in the New Testament that this was the order of events and that thoughts of atonement were simply attached to the death of Jesus by the early church. Rather, the indications are that such thoughts are to be traced back to the mind of Jesus itself.

We may discard at the outset any thought that Jesus, in his sufferings and death, was merely the victim of untoward circumstance, that he fell into the hands of evil conspirators who perpetrated their wicked designs upon a helpless individual. All of the gospel writers make it clear that he went to Jerusalem with his eyes open to the dangers awaiting him there. He did not have to go to Jerusalem; it was by his own choice. He might have saved himself from the agony of the cross. In John's gospel we read: "No one takes it (my life) from me, but I lay it down of my own accord" (10:18). As he told the apostles of the impending dangers awaiting him in Jerusalem, they sought to dissuade him (Mk 8:31–33). They warned him, "The Jews were but now seeking to stone you, and are you going there again?" (Jn 11:8). But their entreaties were turned aside, and "he steadfastly set his face to go to Jerusalem" (Lk 9:51).

We may also dismiss any idea that the death of Jesus was no more than that of a noble martyr willing to die for the truth. Plato, in *The Republic*, has a famous passage in which, by the mouth of Glaucon, there is pictured what the fate of a just man might be expected to be who refuses to compromise his integrity with unjust rulers. The conclusion is:

> The just man will have to endure the lash, the rack, chains, the branding-iron in his eyes, and finally after every extremity of suffering, he will be crucified [literally, "impaled"].[7]

Writers have often compared the fate of Plato's hypothetical just man with the crucifixion of Christ. However, the analogy holds only up to a point. There was something far deeper and more significant in the death of Jesus than the willingness of a just man to endure his fate at the hands of ruthless men rather than to compromise his integrity. We must look beyond this for our answer.

Integral to our inquiry are the following considerations:

(1) The Ransom Word

In Mark 10:45, we have the saying of Jesus, "For the Son of Man also came not to be served but to serve, and to give his life as a ransom for many." This ransom word is sacrificial in character. It occurs in a context where Jesus rebukes James and John for their self-seeking, and calls all of his disciples to a role of humble service. It is to be noted that Jesus did not say that through his death many would be moved to repentance. This might have been true of a martyr's death. The word that Jesus uses carries a meaning quite different from a mere challenge to repentance. It is a sacrificial word, a redemptive word.

There are some scholars who have been all too quick to dismiss the last clause of this verse, with its reference to ransom, as being not from the lips of Jesus but originating in the early church, a post-resurrection addition. Of course there is no way of proving absolutely what Jesus did, or did not, say. But as Professor William Manson so well points out, it fits into the general tenor of Jesus' thought and teachings regarding the Son of Man, and there is no reason to reject this verse as it stands as being an authentic statement of Jesus himself.[8]

(2) The Baptism Word

In Luke 12:49–51, we have three enigmatic statements of Jesus. They may have been spoken on different occasions and brought together by Luke because of their similar tone.

> I came to cast fire upon the earth; and would that it were already kindled! I have a baptism to be baptized with;

and how am I constrained until it is accomplished! Do
you think that I have come to give peace on earth? No, I
tell you, but rather division.

Fire is a symbol of judgment and of conflict, of persecution
and suffering. Thus Peter could speak of "the fiery ordeal" which
his fellow Christians were suffering (1 Pet 4:12). In the Lukan
context above, Jesus was doubtless referring to the fiery ordeal
which he himself would soon undergo.

The reference to his coming baptism carries a similar under-
tone of suffering. Baptism was a metaphor for one who must walk
through deep waters, that is, for one who must undergo some
great trial, possibly involving pain and suffering. The deep waters
of trial must pass over the soul of Jesus, and he longs for the ordeal
to be passed. "Would that it were over!"

He used the baptism metaphor again when he asked James
and John, "Are you able to drink of the cup of which I drink, or to
be baptized with the baptism with which I am baptized?" (Mk
10:38). Clearly, the baptism word was a reference to his approaching suffering and death.

(3) The Covenant Word

The covenant word relates to the sayings of Jesus in the upper
room concerning the new covenant in his blood. It is found in
slightly different form in each of the synoptic gospels and also in
Paul's account of the institution of the Lord's supper in 1 Corinthians 11.

And he took a cup, and when he had given thanks he
gave it to them, and they all drank of it. And he said to
them, "This is my blood of the (new) covenant, which is
poured out for many" (Mk 14:23–24; cf. Mt 26:27–28;
Lk 22:20 footnote; 1 Cor 11:25).

The first part of the sacramental act, the breaking of the
bread, was a symbolic act of sacrifice which every Jew would
understand. The poured-out wine would have reinforced the idea
of sacrifice, representing his life's blood. But more, the blood
becomes the sealing blood of a new covenant. Just as the old
covenant was solemnly sealed with blood (Ex 24), so now the new
covenant which Jesus inaugurates is sealed with his own blood.

One thinks most naturally of the new covenant spoken of by Jeremiah:

Behold, the days are coming, says the Lord, when I will make a new covenant with the house of Israel and the house of Judah, not like the covenant which I made with their fathers when I took them by the hand to bring them out of the land of Egypt, my covenant which they broke. . . . But this is the covenant which I will make with the house of Israel after those days, says the Lord: I will put my law within them, and I will write it upon their hearts; and I will be their God, and they shall be my people . . . for I will forgive their iniquity, and I will remember their sin no more (Jer 31:31–34).

The passage from Jeremiah may indeed have been in the mind of Jesus as he gave the covenant word. In addition, we should look at Deutero-Isaiah, with which Jesus was so familiar, and some of its covenant sayings:

I am the Lord, I have called you in righteousness,
    I have taken you by the hand and kept you;
I have given you as a covenant to the people
    a light to the nations . . . (Is 42:6).

Incline your ear, and come to me;
    hear, that your soul may live;
and I will make with you an everlasting covenant,
    my steadfast, sure love for David (Is 55:3; cf. 49:8–13;
    61:8–9).

Thus in both the writings of Jeremiah and Deutero-Isaiah, we have prophecies of God's intent to establish a new covenant with his people, as they in turn become a blessing to the nations. Jesus saw these promises of a new covenant focusing in on himself. In him the new covenant would be consummated and sealed by his blood.

In his commentary on Luke, Professor William Manson says with reference to the eucharistic cup and the new covenant:

This indicates that under the form of the cup or of the wine within the cup the "new covenant" is given and appropriated. . . . Jesus is conscious that through the

shedding of his blood the new covenant of which prophecy spoke becomes for his followers an accomplished
fact into the benefits of which they now proleptically
enter. His death is not a tragedy simply or a price de-
manded by fidelity to a cause. It is the means of bringing
on, instituting, applying, and sealing a redemption which
by his life and word he has sought to effect but which
only the final sacrifice of his life will bring to fulfillment.
Thus Jesus, according to the evangelical tradition, reads
the final purpose of God in his own mysterious fortunes.[9]

(4) Forewarning Words

We are able to apprehend the mind of Jesus also through his
words of warning to his apostles shortly before his death. At the
retreat in Caesarea Philippi, immediately after Peter's great confession, we read:

> And he began to teach them that the Son of Man must
> suffer many things, and be rejected by the elders and the
> chief priests and the scribes, and be killed, and after
> three days rise again (Mk 8:31).

Mark adds, "And he said this plainly." But the apostles were not
prepared to hear such words. Peter remonstrated with him that
these things must not be. Jesus, in turn, rebuked Peter, seeing in
Peter's words a temptation to take the easy road as distinct from
the way of suffering and death.

In the quotation above "And he began to teach them . . ." the
Greek verb is in the imperfect tense which suggests repeated
action, and indeed the gospel record bears this out. Referring to
the gospel of Mark alone, in the chapters which follow there are a
number of occasions when Jesus repeats his teaching about his
approaching suffering and death (9:12, 31; 10:33–34, 38, 45;
12:7; 14:21).

"Form criticism" tells us that some of the detailed language is
supplied by the early church as post facto history. This is probably
true so far as some of the specific words are concerned. But the
main fact remains that Jesus did not walk blindly to his death; he
foresaw its coming and tried to prepare his apostles for it. Not
only so, but there was a certain divine necessity for it impressed
upon his mind. He felt it was something that he *must* do to fulfill

the divine purpose for him. It was not that he did not cherish his own earthly life, as Gethsemane makes clear. If there could be some other way, as with Abraham and Isaac (Gen 22), he would welcome it. But unless such an alternative was made plain to him, he must not flinch. He must go up to Jerusalem. "He steadfastly set his face . . ." (Lk 9:51).

(5) Prophetic Words

In our consideration of what must have been the mind of Jesus regarding his approaching passion and death, we must weigh the impact of Old Testament prophecies to which he repeatedly appealed. Time and again he spoke of what had been written:

> And he said to them, "Elijah does come first to restore all things; and how is it written of the Son of Man, that he should suffer many things and be treated with contempt?" (Mk 9:12).

> For the Son of Man goes as it is written of him, but woe to that man by whom the Son of Man is betrayed (Mk 14:21).

> And Jesus said to them, "You will all fall away, for it is written, 'I will strike the shepherd, and the sheep will be scattered' " (Mk 14:27).

> And taking the twelve, he said to them, "Behold, we are going up to Jerusalem, and everything that is written of the Son of Man by the prophets will be accomplished" (Lk 18:31).

Among the Old Testament scriptures that Jesus may have had in mind would be the following: Psalms 22; 42:6–11; 69; 124; Zechariah 13:7–9; Isaiah 50:6–9; and preeminently Isaiah 53. Not to take away from the importance of the other scripture passages, Isaiah 53 stands out as the Mount Everest among the mountain peaks. Here the vicarious sufferings and death of a person in behalf of his people are described in detail. Whether the author had in mind as his subject the corporate nation of Israel personified, or a faithful remnant personified, or some individual, has been a matter of much conjecture among theological writers. We do not need to dwell upon this question here. Whatever the original intent of the author, we find in Isaiah 53 a type-event that was to attain its complete fulfillment in the passion, death, and resurrection of Jesus Christ. Luke has preserved a saying of Jesus that bears upon this:

> For I tell you that this scripture must be fulfilled in me, "And he was reckoned with transgressors"; for what is written about me has its fulfillment (22:37).

The New Testament church was quick to see the relationship of Jesus' crucifixion and resurrection to Isaiah 53.[10]

The idea that an individual might bear suffering for the guilt of a corporate people was a part of Jewish theology. Just as the sin of an individual might bring judgment upon the nation as a whole (Jos 7; 2 Sam 24), so the other side of the coin was that an individual might bear the corporate guilt of the nation.

The seeds of this concept are to be found in Moses' plea with God in behalf of the nation, "But now, if thou wilt forgive their sin—and if not, blot me, I pray thee, out of thy book which thou hast written" (Ex 32:32). They are found also in David's plea with God to punish him and his house, but to spare the nation (2 Sam 24:17).

A notable example of the suffering of an individual in behalf of his people is to be found in the experiences of Jeremiah as he took to his own heart the apostasy of the nation:

> My grief is beyond healing,
>   my heart is sick within me. . . .
> For the wound of the daughter of my people
>   is my heart wounded,
> I mourn, and dismay has taken hold on me.
>   Is there no balm in Gilead? . . .
> Oh that my head were waters,
>   and my eyes a fountain of tears,
> that I might weep day and night
>   for the slain of the daughter of my people (Jer 8:18–9:1).

Jeremiah stands as an outstanding example of one who chose to suffer with and for his people. When Jerusalem fell to the

Babylonians, he was invited by the Babylonian commander to go to Babylonia where he would be honored and treated well. He chose instead to remain with the remnant of his people in Judea to share whatever hardship must be endured (Jer 40:1–6). At the same time, while Jeremiah nobly bore Israel's condition as personal pain, there is no suggestion that his suffering was of an expiatory nature.

It remained for Deutero-Isaiah to develop the idea of redemptive suffering, the one for the many, the one bearing the reproaches, griefs, sorrows, and sins of others. This is not simply the idea of one's enduring adversity and profiting from it as good discipline. Such an idea we find in Wisdom literature, and it is basic to Stoic philosophy. The thought in Isaiah 53 is entirely different from this, for here we have the concept of one individual bearing the sin of many as an expiatory sacrifice:

> Surely he has borne our griefs
>   and carried our sorrows;
> Yet we esteemed him stricken,
>   smitten of God and afflicted.
> But he was wounded for our transgressions,
>   he was bruised for our iniquities;
> upon him was the chastisement that made us whole,
>   and with his stripes we are healed.
> All we like sheep have gone astray;
>   we have turned every one to his own way,
> and the Lord has laid on him the iniquity of us all. . . .
> When he makes himself an offering (*asham*) for sin,
>   he shall see his offspring, he shall prolong his days;
> the will of the Lord shall prosper in his hand. . . .
> By his knowledge (sufferings)[11] shall the righteous one, my
>   servant,
>   make many to be accounted righteous,
>   and he shall bear their iniquities (Is 53:4–11).[12]

It is to be noted in verse 10 that the servant offers his life as an *asham*, a guilt offering, the familiar Jewish sacrifice of expiation. The sacrifice is followed by the servant's exaltation. One of the servant's rewards is the satisfaction of seeing the fruit of the travail of his soul whereby many are to be accounted righteous. The term "many," which is used twice in this passage, was a Jewish expression denoting the larger community of nations, Gentiles as well as Jews (cf. 49:6 and 52:15). The servant's other reward is the approval of God. It is God's pleasure to reward him by "lifting him up" and giving him "a portion with the great" (52:13; 53:12).

It would seem to be self-evident that Isaiah 53 was very much a part of the thinking of Jesus as he made his most crucial decision. We have already observed how he identified himself with the servant of Deutero-Isaiah. Was it enough for him to do so in his manner of living, but not in his death? Was not his teaching about the kingdom of God, his genuine concern for others, his healing ministry, and his training of the twelve sufficient to win the world to God? No, if he was to accept the role of servant, it must be the full script; he must follow it all the way, including the expiatory sacrifice. Nothing less than offering his life as an *asham* would lift the many to God.

The way would not be easy, for he loved life with all the purity of his being, and he loved those around him, fallible and unstable though they were. But he saw this as God's will for him and he must not flinch from it. If this was the Father's will, then he (Christ) would be supported in his ordeal by the Father. It is interesting to compare this situation with other words concerning the servant:

> The Lord God has opened my ear,
>   and I was not rebellious,
>   I turned not backward.
> I gave my back to the smiters,
>   and my cheeks to those who pulled out the beard;
> I hid not my face
>   from shame and spitting.
> For the Lord God helps me;
>   therefore I have not been confounded;
> therefore I have set my face like a flint,
>   and I know that I shall not be put to shame;
>   he who vindicates me is near (Is 50:6–8).

From all of the foregoing considerations, we are led to conclude that Jesus, in his own mind, looked upon his impending death as an expiatory sacrifice, "a ransom for many"; and he envisioned that by his sacrifice a new covenant would be established and sealed by his blood.

But Why Not Simple Forgiveness?

The question needs to be dealt with forthrightly: Why not simple forgiveness? Why do we need to bother with a process of expiation, or atonement? The argument would run somewhat as follows: In our enlightened age, we believe God to be a God of love and compassion. He is not out to get us; he has no interest in punishment or retribution. Forgiveness is an act of total grace. One of the most beautiful stories in the New Testament is the narrative about the prodigal son. He came back with nothing in his pockets, and his father forgave him. Nothing was said about working out the debt in the fields, nothing about an expiation offering. The forgiveness was all grace.

As concerns the prodigal son, it needs to be pointed out that the story is in the form of a parable, and a parable is designed to teach some one great truth, in this case the father's willingness to forgive the penitent, which means God's willingness. But it is dangerous to try to pin a total gospel on one segment of scripture. It is total scripture that makes up the gospel as we interpret scripture with scripture. What appears to be simple forgiveness may not be the total gospel.

Another part of the answer to keep before ourselves is the fact that expiation has to do with the annulment of sin and guilt, which is on man's side; it is not to be regarded as a propitiation of God. It is man who needs it, not God. Expiation is prescribed by God on man's behalf, not for God's benefit. Reconciliation is always of man to God, not God to man.

We need to look at the issue from another angle also, and this is the crux of the matter: real forgiveness is never cheap or easy and should never be so regarded. To refer again to the story of the prodigal son, and reading between the lines, the father must have suffered untold agony of heart for many days during the absence of his lost son. His seeing his son on the road "while he was yet at a distance" suggests this. His forgiveness, therefore, must have come out of much travail.

A forgiveness in words, that costs nothing, is superficial and shallow. It is debatable whether it is forgiveness at all. Without cost, it becomes meaningless both to the giver and to the receiver. It does not heal but, on the contrary, leaves a festering wound.

Professor Donald Baillie gives an illustration of two friends, one of whom in a moment of weakness plays false to his friend, behind his back, betraying his friend's confidence. When the other hears about it, will he pass it off lightly as though it does not matter? When the offender comes in deep distress and attempts to apologize, will the other treat it casually for the sake of comfortable relations? This he cannot do if he is a true friend and cares deeply; he will accept his deep hurt as he forgives. His forgiveness will not be shallow; it will not be good-natured indulgence. It will emerge out of both love and pain. Only thus can forgiveness be genuine and significant.[13] Professor Baillie adds:

> He (God) cannot take our sins lightly or treat them with indulgence. . . . God must be inexorable towards our sins; not because he is just, but because he is loving; not in spite of his love, but because of his love.[14]

Such forgiveness, coming out of suffering love as a consuming fire, burns away the sin and dross and leaves only purity of soul. Such forgiveness has atonement as its basis and issues in unspeakable gratitude, joy, and peace.

The *asham* sacrifice represented such a costly offering for sin. In it, the offrant expressed symbolically genuine pain and sorrow for sin, coincident with self-giving to God. It said symbolically that sin does matter and that its "covering" (annulment) is costly. This is why simple forgiveness is not enough. Atonement is inherent in forgiveness.

St. Paul's Views of the Atonement

We turn now to St. Paul's views of the atonement. We believe that his views also correctly reflect the teachings of the early church. Unfortunately the apostle did not leave behind a systematic treatise on the subject. Had he done so, he would have saved theologians a great deal of trouble and, incidentally, the world a great deal of ink! It is more correct to speak of his *views* of the atonement than his view of it, for he uses a number of metaphors to describe it. However, as we examine the different metaphors, we find that they reinforce each other and form a mosaic with a fairly clear picture.

A presentation of the terms used by Paul is in itself not absolutely decisive, because our interpretation of these terms depends in part on their connotation in the Old Testament and partly on the new meaning put into them by Paul and by others in the New Testament church, and on these points there is some variance of opinions among theologians. The main thing to keep in mind is that behind all of the metaphors used by Paul, there is a reality, and the sum of that reality is the cancellation of our sins and our acceptance into fellowship with God.

Paul's views of the atonement may be summarized under six headings, most of them derived from the metaphors that he used to describe it. In many sentences or paragraphs, the metaphors, two or more, occur side by side.

(1) Atonement Means Redemption

The Greek term is *apolutrosis*. The root verb is *lutroo* which means to set free by payment of a ransom. We are reminded of Jesus' well-known statement: "For the Son of Man came not to be served but to serve, and to give his life as a ransom for many" (Mk 10:45). The result of such action is redemption. In the Old Testament a good illustration of redemption is the act of Hosea who found his wife on the auction block about to be sold as a slave and bought her back by paying the purchase price (Hos 3).

However, there are other times when the term is used in the sense of emancipation without specific reference to a purchase price. Israel was said to have been redeemed from Egypt. God is often referred to as Israel's redeemer. This was a favorite title with Deutero-Isaiah to indicate God's relationship to Israel.

It is natural that such thoughts should be carried over into the New Testament, only now it is Christ who becomes the redeemer through the purchase price of his own blood. Therefore Christians are not their own; they are "bought with a price" (1 Cor 6:19–20; 7:23). In Paul's writings, Christians are pictured as set free by Christ from the bondage of sin (Rom 6:18–20), from bondage to the law (Romans and Galatians), and from the power of death (1 Cor 15:55–57).

In Romans Paul presents the beautiful paradoxical thought that those who were once in bondage to sin are now set free, and have become slaves of righteousness, slaves of God (6:17–22). In like manner, Paul regarded himself as emancipated from bondage to sin, to the law, and to the power of death, yet referred to himself repeatedly as "the bondslave of Jesus Christ" (Rom 1:1 and elsewhere).[15]

(2) Atonement Means Justification

The Greek term is *dikaiosune*. The verb to justify, and the nouns justice, justification, and righteousness, are all derived from the same root and are among the most frequently used words in scripture. Justice and righteousness, for all practical purposes, are synonymous as used in scripture and point to the same condition. One might say that justice is the process and righteousness the resulting state.

God is just and righteous in his being and requires justice and righteousness of his people. When justice toward one's fellow man is violated, then the righteousness of God is violated. The call of the prophets, in the name of God, was for justice. One of the marks of the messiah was that his rule would be with justice and with righteousness (Is 9:7; 11:4).

It follows that any act of injustice, or state of injustice, is a violation of God's order and therefore is subject to his judgment. This brings in the figure of the courtroom. God sits as judge of his people. By all counts, sinful men before the divine tribunal stand condemned. Yet the paradox is that because of the righteousness of Christ and man's faith in him, the sinner is pronounced "not guilty," and is set free. He is justified by faith in Christ whose righteousness is accepted in his stead. This would seem to make a travesty of justice except for the sinner's identification with Christ who has met the absolute requirement of righteousness. The following is a part of Paul's presentation of the case:

> For no human being will be justified in his sight by works of the law. . . . But now the righteousness of God has been manifested apart from the law, although the law and the prophets bear witness to it, the righteousness of God through faith in Jesus Christ for all who believe. For there is no distinction; since all have sinned and fall short of the glory of God, they are justified by his grace as a gift, through the redemption which is in Christ Jesus, whom God put forward as an expiation by his blood, to be received by faith. This was to show God's righteousness, because in his divine forbearance he had passed over former sins; it was to prove at the present time that he himself is righteous and that he justifies him who has faith in Jesus (Rom 3:20–26).

The transmission of righteousness to the sinner is not mechanical. It is implied, or specifically stated elsewhere, that the nature of the sinner is changed. A transformation takes place so that the person becomes "a new creation" in Christ (2 Cor 5:17).

This is made clear also in Romans: "So you also must consider yourselves dead to sin and alive to God in Christ Jesus" (6:11).

Thus the justification imputed by Christ becomes the instrument, or the occasion, of moral and spiritual renewal. Therefore, this writer cannot agree with those who contend that justification in the New Testament sense is immoral because it lets the sinner "off the hook." On the contrary, it makes justification (salvation) an act of grace, pure grace, and therein the sinner is both reclaimed and transformed, which is God's purpose.[16]

(3) Atonement Means Reconciliation

The Greek term is *katallage*. The fundamental effect of sin is conceived in scripture as separation and estrangement from God. In the Genesis story of the fall, after Adam and Eve had eaten of the forbidden fruit, "they hid themselves from the presence of the Lord God among the trees of the garden (Gen 3:8). If the effect of sin is estrangement from God, or enmity toward God, then the chief need of man is the elimination of the cause, which is sin, and the reestablishment of fellowship with God. This, according to Paul, is what Christ accomplished for us through his atoning death.

We think naturally of Paul's classic passage on reconciliation in 2 Corinthians:

> All this is from God, who through Christ reconciled us to himself and gave us the ministry of reconciliation; that is, God was in Christ reconciling the world to himself, not counting their trespasses against them, and entrusting to us the message of reconciliation. So we are ambassadors for Christ, God making his appeal through us. We beseech you on behalf of Christ: be reconciled to God (5:18–20).

Of particular interest to us is a passage in Colossians where reconciliation is linked to *pleroma:*

> For in him all the fullness (*pleroma*) of God was pleased to dwell, and through him to reconcile to himself all things, whether on earth or in heaven, making peace by the blood of his cross. And you, who were once estranged and hostile in mind, doing evil deeds, he has now

reconciled in the body of his flesh by his death, in order to present you holy and blameless and irreproachable before him (1:19–22; cf. Rom 5:10–11).

Paul conceives of the reconciliation as both personal and cosmic. It is to be emphasized that the reconciliation in all cases is of man to God, not God to man. The fact that it is God who has taken the initiative and provided the means of reconciliation is proof that it is not he, but man, who needs to be reconciled. It is man who, by disobedience, has separated himself from God and erected a barrier between himself and God. The irony of the situation is that man's nature has become so corrupted and weakened by sin that his only hope is that God will be merciful and come to him. It is God who must bridge the gap. This, according to scripture, is precisely what he has done. In Christ, he has crossed over the chasm. The barrier erected by man by his disobedience, he has removed. In Christ, God and man are "at-one," which is atonement.[17]

(4) Atonement Means Expiation

The Greek word is *hilasterion.* We have already surveyed the Old Testament use of this term. Professor C.H. Dodd, who has done a thorough research of this word, says that whereas it is used by some pagan writers in the sense of placating a man or a god, this meaning is practically unknown in the Septuagint where it means to perform an act (such as the payment of a fine or the offering of a sacrifice) by which sin and guilt are annulled.[18]

The expiation sacrifice was regarded as a means which God himself had appointed for the blotting out, or annulling, of sin and guilt. It was God's gift of mercy to man. The sinner's part was to identify himself with the sacrifice. The expiation offering, therefore, was not to be looked upon as propitiatory, but as God's provision whereby sin and guilt were cancelled. This is generally recognized by scholars, and the Revised Standard Version has correctly translated the word as expiation rather than propitiation (Rom 3:25; 1 Jn 2:2; 4:10).

Beyond this, however, there is a wide variation of interpretations as to how the death of Jesus on the cross effects atonement:

■ Some regard the crucifixion as Christ's bearing the equivalent judgment and punishment that otherwise would be the sinner's due.

- Some see his death as the means of satisfying the requirements of divine holiness and justice.
- Some interpret his death as an act of perfect obedience which God accepts in our behalf as we identify ourselves with his act by faith.
- Some say that since Christ has identified himself with humanity, his sacrifice was therefore representative in nature, vicarious and substitutionary. Consequently it can be rightly said that Christ died "for us," "in our behalf," and "for our sins" —yet not in the sense of punishment.
- Still others see in Christ's death the supreme example of God's love which both pronounces judgment upon sin and motivates the sinner to respond in penitence, gratitude, and dedication.

A true interpretation probably involves a combination of most of the above ideas, though the first two would be rejected by many scholars, or would need further refinement and clarification. Paul's concept would certainly include the following:

(1) That Christ's death is to be thought of as an expiatory sacrifice (Rom 3:25).
(2) That Christ died for the remission of our sins (1 Cor 15:3; Col 1:14).
(3) That Christ, by his death, is to be regarded as our paschal lamb, which implies redemption (1 Cor 5:7). Also, it is of note that in point of time the apostle Paul records the first account of the establishing of the eucharist where sacrificial language is used (1 Cor 11:23–26).
(4) That Christ bore sin's curse in our stead (Gal 3:13).
(5) That Christ's death has redeeming power for all who identify with it by faith (Rom 3:24–25; Col 1:14).

(5) Atonement Means Victory

The key Greek word is *nikos,* which is translated victory. It has the idea of having been victorious over one's enemies. Two passages in Colossians are especially pertinent:

He delivered us from the dominion of darkness and transferred us to the kingdom of his beloved Son (1:14; cf. Rom 7:24–25; 8:37; 1 Cor 15:57).

He disarmed the principalities and powers and made a
public example of them, triumphing over them in him
(or, "in it," the cross) (2:15).

This concept, sometimes called the "classic view of the
atonement," envisions the struggle against evil forces as being
cosmic in scope, of which the earthly struggle is but one front.
These evil forces, inhabiting the upper regions of the universe,
especially the planets and stars, seek to impose their deceitful
wiles on men, subjecting them to bondage, disease, disasters of
various kinds, sin, and death. (See Chapter 2)

According to this view of the atonement, the evil powers did
their worst at the cross, but physical death was the utmost that
they could inflict on Jesus; they could not break his spirit. In very
picturesque language the apostle Paul envisions Jesus as seizing
the hammer from the evil powers and nailing sin's accusations to
the cross, thus cancelling them (Col 2:14). He (Christ) then disarmed the evil powers and led them captive-bound behind his
triumphal chariot (the cross). All of this is vividly portrayed in
Colossians 2:14–15. The English translation does not convey the
full picture and force of the Greek on these points.

The "classic view" of the atonement has been presented and
defended in detail in Bishop Gustaf Aulen's book, *Christus Victor.*
This view doubtless holds an important truth, but not the whole
truth as Bishop Aulen seems to maintain. There is comfort and
assurance in the realization that Jesus, both in his life and death,
overcame the forces of evil, however they are to be conceived,
and passes on his victory to all who are united with him by faith.

(6) Atonement Means Participation in Eternal Life

This concept turns not so much upon a single word, as being a
theme that runs through all of Paul's epistles and the New Testament in general. With the certainty of eternal life shared with
Christ, Paul looks upon death, not with dread, but with expectation; as an opportunity "to depart and be with Christ" (Phil 1:23).

While there are many passages that might be cited that depict
this resurrection hope, we shall content ourselves with two which
may be said to be typical:

But now that you have been set free from sin and have
become slaves of God, the return you get is sanctification

and its end, eternal life. For the wages of sin is death, but
the free gift of God is eternal life in Jesus Christ our Lord
(Rom 6:22–23).

But our commonwealth (colony) is in heaven and from it
we await a Savior, the Lord Jesus Christ, who will change
our lowly body to be like his glorious body, by the power
which enables him even to subject all things to himself
(Phil 3:20–21).[19]

Life in Christ, the source of the Christian's blessedness on
earth, is extended as eternal life in the world to come. The resurrection glory of Christ, which will be shared by all Christians, will
be a state of blessedness that is beyond human conception (1
Cor 2:9).

Two Axiomatic Truths

There are two important truths which are axiomatic to the
atonement:

(1) *The first is that the atonement must be complete and absolute.* In contrast to a sacrifice which may be partial and transitory,
or individualistic, the sacrifice for mankind must be absolute and
adequate for all.

The writer to the Hebrews makes this very point as he compares the transitoriness of the Aaronic sacrifices with that offered
by Christ (7:23–28, 10:10–14). Likewise, in the mind of Paul,
there is never the slightest doubt of the ultimate nature of Christ's
sacrifice, and that for the reason: "For in him all the fullness of
God was pleased to dwell" (Col 1:19; cf. 2:9). In contrast to the
false teachers at Colossae who apparently were saying that
Christ's redemption from sin was partial and inadequate, Paul said
that on the contrary it was full and complete and represented
nothing less than the "fullness of God" in his self-giving. There
was never the slightest doubt in Paul's mind of the absolute nature
of Christ's sacrifice. Therefore the sacrifice had the nature of
being final, "once for all" (Rom 6:10; cf. Heb 7:27; 9:12; 10:10; 1
Pet 3:18).

It was this that made all the difference between his death and
that of any noble martyr. Here was a person who was not merely
mystically conscious of God's presence, or a man so filled with the
Holy Spirit as to reveal the nature of God, or a man who so

exemplified God's love in caring service as to take on the religious value of God. However well intended, such remarks fall short of interpreting the mind of Paul. Such views, while they may sound plausible and even have a popular appeal, are consigned to transiency, for sinful men seeking relief from a sense of guilt will always come back asking for more than the example of a good and great man. They will need, and demand, an atonement that is absolute and ultimate. This they will find in St. Paul's Christ "in whom all the fullness of God was pleased to dwell" (Col 1:19), "who gave himself for our sins" (Gal 1:4; 1 Cor 15:3).

(2) *The second important truth is that the atonement had to take place from within humanity.* The *"kenosis* narrative" in Philippians declares that this is precisely what happened. While the atonement was all God's act of grace and by his own initiative, as he did for us what we could never do for ourselves, nevertheless it was not an act of God per se, but of the God-man. The offering, while from God, was also to him, from within our humanity. Nor was the manhood merely instrumental, but integral to the procedure.

> For God has done what the law, weakened by the flesh, could not do: sending his own Son in the likeness of sinful flesh and for sin (as a sin offering), he condemned sin in the flesh (Rom 8:3).

Paul never tires of emphasizing the historic nature of the atonement.[20] All of the Adam comparisons are based on the fact that Christ, as the "second Adam," took upon himself the flesh of the "first Adam," and reversed the sinful process.[21] As was true with the Old Testament sacrificial system, that man, the offender, made an offering to God, though it was a provision of God in man's behalf, so when the supreme sacrifice was made, it was from the human side Godward. It was "in the form of a servant . . . in the likeness of men" that the sacrifice was offered.

The writer to the Hebrews makes it a point of strong emphasis that it was from within our humanity that Christ made his sacrifice:

> Since therefore the children share in flesh and blood, he himself likewise partook of the same nature. . . . For surely it is not with angels that he is concerned but with the descendants of Abraham. Therefore he had to be

made like his brethren in every respect so that he might become a merciful and faithful high priest in the service of God, to make expiation for the sins of the people (2:14–17).

In like manner, Paul never loses sight of the human side of the sacrifice. It was "Jesus Christ, descended from David according to the flesh" (Rom 1:3), "whom God put forward as an expiation by his blood, to be received by faith" (Rom 3:24–25). Being fully identified with us according to the flesh, he is fully qualified to be our representative before God.

Thus, any true apprehension and appreciation of the atonement combine the two requisites: its absoluteness, and its movement from human need Godward.

6

The Relevance of the Paradox to the Church

I shall pray for the Church, my God, each day during the celebration of the Eucharist. My faith can only survive in the community of those who together form the holy Church of Jesus Christ. . . . Truthfully though, I do not consider myself to be any better than others in the Church; I know that I am anything but a sterling argument for the origin of the Church in the mercy of God's will, I who am a member of this Church and am supposed to represent it. . . . God, have mercy upon us poor, short-sighted, and foolish sinners, we who form the body of Your Church. . . . I must confess that I see these miracles (of divine grace) more plainly among the young people in the Church (Andrea, for instance, who worked for an entire year without pay as a laundress in a home for abandoned youths during the course of her studies) than among the adults whose comfortable, middle-class existence goes its inevitable way. But perhaps my weary eyes do not allow me to view "authority" and "power" without becoming unduly emotional. . . . One may, in all good conscience, sing praises to the sanctity of the Church. It professes for all times Your divine grace and Your unspeakable grandeur above and beyond anything which can be imagined. . . . Even a somewhat bitter lament and a plea for divine mercy toward the Church still praise this Church and Your mercy. (Excerpts from "Prayer for the Church," Karl Rahner, *Prayers for a Lifetime,* 114–117)

The Church Defined

The New Testament word for church is *ekklesia,* which means literally those "called out," and hence an assembly. It was the

113

word used by the Greeks and Romans for a public assembly called to consider some current issue or to hear an official announcement. It was also the word used in the Septuagint for assembly or congregation. From it comes our English word "ecclesiastical." It is an interesting and significant thought that Christians are "a people called out" by Christ to be his disciples—"called out" from the world, then "sent" back into the world as his ambassadors of reconciliation.

Paul's Lofty View of the Church

Paul's high Christology (Chapter 2) is linked to his lofty view of the church. The two are conjoined and cannot be separated.

Nowhere do we find this more substantiated than in the letter to the Ephesians. Scholars are divided as to whether Ephesians was written by Paul himself or by a later disciple of Paul. The arguments and evidence for each viewpoint can be traced in good commentaries. All things considered, this writer abides by the traditional view of Pauline authorship, or at the very least that the epistle correctly reflects the mind and spirit of the apostle.

Ephesians has been called an "ecclesiastical epistle" because in it, as in no other New Testament writing, we have presented the doctrine of the church. If in Colossians Paul holds up before us the person of Christ, in Ephesians he holds up before us the church.

The Transcendent As Well As the Visible Church

To fully appreciate Paul's understanding of the church, we have to transport ourselves in thought, with Paul, above the historical level to the transcendent church as it exists in the thought and purpose of God. With Paul we stand on a mountaintop, as it were, where we are able to see the church in its larger perspectives, high above the church nestled in the valley below. Yet, within the transcendent vision, the church in the valley, with all of its weaknesses, foibles, and problems, is never forgotten. On the contrary, it is the very instrument of God for fulfilling his purpose. It is within the historical church that God's grace abounds and from which the divine light shines as from earthen vessels.

The starting point in perceiving the true nature of the church is the recognition that the church is not a human institution, but a divine one. It does not exist because a few people decide to organize themselves into a worshiping community. What people do in this regard is incidental to, and derivative from, the working of the Spirit of God who calls forth a people as his own, redeems them in Christ, and commissions them to carry out his sovereign purpose in the world.

The historical church, therefore, is never to be assessed solely by its outward manifestation. It is a spiritual entity, mystically united with Christ and empowered by the Holy Spirit to convey Christ's work of redemption. On the historical level, it is the recipient of God's gifts and graces, which are the "earnest" (down-payment) of the blessedness in the world to come.

Four Pictures of the Church

Paul's views of the church are best seen by examining the metaphors which he uses concerning it. There are four major ones:

(1) *The church is the people of God.* In the Old Testament, Israel was spoken of as God's own people. This is stated in many places and in different ways, of which the following are samples:

> Say therefore to the people of Israel, "I am the Lord, and I will bring you out from under the burdens of the Egyptians . . . and I will take you for my people, and I will be your God" (Ex 6:6–7).

> Now, therefore, if you will obey my voice and keep my covenant, you shall be my own possession among all peoples (Ex 19:5).

> For the Lord's portion is his people, Jacob his allotted heritage (Dt 32:9; cf. 9:26, 29; Zech 2:12).[1]

Israel is God's family, his very own people. They are not only the descendants of Abraham, Isaac and Jacob, but the children of God. However rebellious they might prove to be at times, they are still his children, called upon to repent and return to him (Is 1:2; Jer 3:14; and numerous other places).

The New Testament picks up on these terms and uses them of the church. The church is the new "Israel of God" (Gal 6:16). More correctly it is the continuing Israel, in line with the promises made to Abraham, Moses and others.

> If you are Christ's, then you are Abraham's offspring,
> heirs according to promise (Gal 3:29).

God's own portion is "his glorious inheritance in the saints" (Eph 1:18). With this, we should compare Ephesians 1:11–12:

> In him we were chosen as his inheritance, being predes-
> tined, according to the purpose of him who accomplishes
> all things according to the counsel of his will, to live to
> the praise of his glory, we who first hoped in Christ.[2]

This is a beautiful thought, that God's glorious inheritance is in his saints. Some commentators, however, seem reluctant to accept this meaning and work around it to make it refer to the glorious inheritance *of the saints,* in keeping with teachings in some other places (e.g. Eph 1:14; Rom 8:17). However, the Greek rendition seems clear enough that God's glorious inheritance is *in his saints,* and this is in perfect harmony with the Old Testament teaching, "The Lord's portion is his people, Jacob his allotted heritage" (Dt 32:9).

It is precisely here that the church is both cautioned and challenged. Israel as a whole came to look upon her election as a call to privilege, something that set her apart from other nations as favored and better than they. She forgot that she had been chosen for service. In his call to Abraham, God said:

> I will make you a great nation, and I will bless you, and
> make your name great, so that you will be a blessing . . .
> and by you all the families of the earth will be blessed
> (Gen 12:2–3).

In the same vein, in the covenant made to Moses, God said of Israel:

> Now therefore, if you will obey my voice and keep my
> covenant, you shall be my possession among all peoples;
> for all the earth is mine, and you shall be to me a kingdom
> of priests and a holy nation (Ex 19:5–6).

A kingdom of priests is a reference to Israel's mission. A priest is one who ministers to others in the name of God, and is a mediator on man's behalf before God. To be a priest means just the opposite of being set apart to privilege, except as service to one's fellow men in the name of God should always be considered a privilege. Israel forgot her mission.

Peter, with the Exodus passage in mind, wrote to his fellow Christians:

> But you are a chosen race, a royal priesthood, a holy nation, God's own people, that you may declare the wonderful deeds of him who called you out of darkness into his marvelous light (1 Pet 2:9).

The words are Peter's, transferring the terms of the first covenant to the new Israel, but they also express the substance of Paul's thought as well. We are the family and household of God, his very own people, a kingdom of priests, his ambassadors of reconciliation called and set apart by him to declare his wonderful deeds, most specifically his immeasurable love and unspeakable grace in his Son, Jesus Christ. Israel forgot her true mission; the new Israel must not forget!

(2) *The church is the building or temple of God.* The church is "a holy temple, a dwelling place of God in the Spirit" (Eph 2:19–22).

In 1 Corinthians, as Paul deals with the problem of immorality, he appeals for chaste living on the ground that the human body is a temple of the living God, the dwelling place of the Spirit, and therefore should be kept holy (3:16; 6:19). In Ephesians, the thought changes somewhat and it is the corporate people of God who are the holy temple.

In 1 Corinthians, where the church is also likened to a building, Christ is declared to be the foundation (3:10–11). But in Ephesians the figure changes and the apostles and prophets become the foundation, with Christ the chief cornerstone. The chief cornerstone, which today is known as the keystone, was in Paul's day the stone at the top of an arch which held the arch in place and gave unity to the whole. The members of the church are fitted and joined together, with Christ the chief cornerstone holding all together in unity.

We cannot but be reminded of Peter's analogy of the church as a temple of God:

> Come to him, to that living stone, rejected by men but in God's sight chosen and precious; and like living stones be

yourselves built into a spiritual house, to be a holy
priesthood, to offer spiritual sacrifices to God through
Jesus Christ (1 Pet 2:4–5).

Paul and Peter had in mind something quite different from
material buildings when they likened the church to a temple of
God. They were envisioning the people of God as a spiritual temple, indwelt by the Spirit of God. It is interesting that whereas
today we so often associate the local church with a building or
buildings, for over three centuries, so far as we can trace, there
were no church buildings. Not until the time of Constantine,
when Christianity was adopted officially as the religion of the
empire, did church buildings, as such, begin to appear.

(3) *The church is the bride of Christ.* Of all the figures of the
church, this one is doubtless the most beautiful and appealing:

Husbands, love your wives, as Christ loved the church
and gave himself up for her, that he might sanctify her,
having cleansed her by the washing of water with the
word, that he might present the church to himself in
splendor, without spot or wrinkle or any such thing, that
she might be holy and without blemish (Eph 5:25–27).

Sometimes in the course of a lecture, or a section of a book,
an illustration may prove to be more interesting and of more value
than the main point that is being pursued. So it is here. The
essential thrust of this passage is to remind husbands and wives of
what their mutual relationship should be. As a shining example,
he cites the relationship between Christ and his church.

The metaphor has its roots in the Old Testament. In a number
of places, Israel is likened to the wife of the Lord. The following
will serve as examples:

For your Maker is your husband,
   the Lord of hosts is his name (Is 54:5).

As a bridegroom rejoices over the bride,
   so shall God rejoice over you (Is 62:5).

And in that day, says the Lord, you will call me "My
husband" . . . and I will betroth you to me forever; I will
betroth you to me in righteousness and in justice,
in steadfast love and in mercy. I will betroth you to

me in faithfulness; and you shall know the Lord (Hos 2:16–20).[3]

In several passages, God is spoken of as "a jealous God."[4] The basis for his jealousy is that Israel is thought of as his spouse, whom he is unwilling to share with false gods. Likewise, there are many passages where Israel's unfaithfulness is characterized as that of an unfaithful wife who plays the harlot.[5]

The picture of Christ as the bridegroom may be traced to discourses of Jesus himself. When he was asked why he and his disciples did not fast, as did the disciples of John the Baptist and the Pharisees, he replied, "Can the wedding guests fast while the bridegroom is with them? As long as they have the bridegroom with them, they cannot fast" (Mk 2:19). Also the bridegroom figure was used in some of his parables where the natural reference was to himself.[6]

John the Baptist, in like manner, speaks of Jesus as the bridegroom:

You yourselves bear me witness, that I said, I am not the Christ, but I have been sent before him. He who has the bride is the bridegroom; the friend of the bridegroom, who stands and hears him, rejoices greatly at the bridegroom's voice; therefore this joy of mine is now full (Jn 3:28–30).

Returning to the Ephesians' passage, it is stated that Christ cleanses and sanctifies the church by the washing of water with the word. The washing with water was probably a reference to Christian baptism. The mention of the word reminds us that in scripture the word of God was thought of as having a purifying effect.[7] In both Roman and Jewish traditions, it was customary that the bride, on her wedding day, be given her "bridal bath." This was so much the standard procedure that the "bridal bath" was considered virtually a part of the wedding day ritual. This was doubtless in the background of Paul's mind as he talked about the cleansing and sanctification of the church.

The bride is then dressed in her finest garments, which are "without spot or wrinkle or any such thing." Subsequently, as she stands beside the bridegroom, she is "holy and without blemish." Certainly this is a most beautiful picture of the relationship of Christ and his church!

A passage from Genesis is recalled by Paul to suggest the oneness of the union: "For this reason a man shall leave his father and mother and be joined to his wife, and the two shall become one" (Gen 2:24). Paul adds, "This is a great mystery, and I take it to mean Christ and the church." The joining of two lives as one in holy marriage is indeed a great mystery, yet a glorious reality for all who experience it. The mystical union of Christ and his church is also a great mystery and a glorious reality!

(4) *The church is the body of Christ.* Judging by the many times this figure is used, it was Paul's favorite metaphor. If the figure of the church as the bride of Christ is the most beautiful, the metaphor of the church as the body of Christ is the most apt and significant. It is the only figure of speech which we have considered that does not have its roots in the Old Testament. The precise origin of it is unknown; a number of theories have been suggested.[8] However, it may have originated with Paul himself.

Among a number of passages, the theme is developed most fully in the twelfth chapter of 1 Corinthians.

For just as the body is one and has many members, and
all the members of the body, though many, are one body,
so it is with Christ (1 Cor 12:12).

One would expect Paul to have said, "So it is with the church." Instead, he says, "So it is with Christ." To Paul, the church as the body of Christ is more than a mere figure of speech. The church is not compared to a body; the church *is* in a real sense the mystical body of Christ.[9] As in his incarnate life Christ had to have a body in which to proclaim his message and to do his work, so now the risen and exalted Lord has to have a body through which to express his thought and to do his work in the world. This he does through the community of believers, the church.

We miss the point if we conceive of the community of believers merely as those who have been captivated by the ideals of Jesus and want now to emulate and perpetuate them. Certainly idealism would be included, but idealism only touches the fringe of the reality. Rather, the Spirit of the risen Christ pervades his church and vitalizes it. His living presence animates his church. The church is filled with his fullness.

If one asks how the risen Christ can be at the right hand of the Father and at the same time so intimately present in his church, the answer lies in the gift of the Holy Spirit whom Jesus promised to send (Jn 14:16, 26; 16:7). While the three persons of the Trinity are distinguished in the scriptures, nevertheless they cannot be separated in experience. As another has said, "One cannot have one member of the Trinity without having all three."[10] As an example, consider the movement from one person to another in the following passage:

> Now there are varieties of gifts, but the same Spirit; and there are varieties of service, but the same Lord; and there are varieties of working, but it is the same God who inspires them all in every one (1 Cor 12:4–5).

In this chapter dealing with the church as the body of Christ, the affinity of Christ and the Holy Spirit is clearly exhibited. "No one can say 'Jesus is Lord' except by the Holy Spirit" (12:3). The many and varied gifts bestowed upon the disciples are gifts of the Spirit. It is the Spirit who brings unity to the church:

> For by one Spirit we were all baptized into one body, Jews or Greeks, slaves or free—and all were made to drink of one Spirit (12:13).

It is the Spirit who animates and empowers the church. Just as the human body would be lifeless without the human spirit, so the church would be lifeless without the inbreathing of the Holy Spirit.

In Romans 12:4–8, the same teaching about the church as the body of Christ is given in summary form. In neither 1 Corinthians nor Romans is there a distinction made between the head and the body, but rather, together, they are thought of as the body of Christ. In fact, in 1 Corinthians, the ear, the eye, and the sense of smell are specifically mentioned as necessary parts of the body (12:16–17). But when we come to Colossians, which was written at a later date, when Paul had occasion to stress the Lordship of Christ, in opposition to the false teachers, he makes a distinction between the head and the body. In Colossians, Christ is sovereign Lord over all creation and "head of the body, the church" (1:15–18; 2:19). In Ephesians, likewise, the sovereignty of Christ is stressed and he is presented as "the head of the church, which is his body" (1:23; 4:12; 5:30).

In Paul's day the head was considered to be not only the control-center from which the body took its directions, but also the source of all the vital life forces, supplying the body with all the necessary requirements for nurture and growth. With this in mind, the apostle encourages the church to continue to develop and grow in faith and in the knowledge of the Son of God "to mature manhood, to the measure of the stature of the fullness of Christ" (Eph 4:13). We are to "grow up in every way into him who is the head, into Christ" (Eph 4:15).

The church as the body of Christ is the continuing incarnation in the world. We are solemnly charged with the commission to proclaim the good news of the kingdom of God to all nations and to perform the works of his kingdom. He is counting on us, in fact is dependent on our faithfulness. As he has not failed us, so we must not fail him! We are his hands to do his works, his feet to run his errands, his mouthpiece to speak his words of eternal life. We are his body!

The Fullness (Pleroma) of the Church

We come now to consider the important and captivating passage in Ephesians where "fullness" (pleroma) is used with reference to the church. The passage reads as follows:

> And he (God) has put all things under his feet (Christ's) and made him the head over all things for the church, which is his body, the fullness (*pleroma*) of him who fills all in all (Eph 1:22–23).

The passage is a difficult one. It occurs within the context of Paul's statement regarding the exaltation of Christ to the right hand of God and his (Christ's) being given sovereignty over all things. The last clause, "who fills all in all," was a well-known expression to denote the universal presence of God. Only here, it is used as appertaining to Christ.

The church, "his body," is said to be "the fullness (*pleroma*) of him (Christ) who fills all in all." The proper interpretation of "fullness" (pleroma) as used here depends on whether the word is to be understood in an active sense or in a passive sense. Ordinarily and as a general rule *pleroma* would be understood as passive, but there are exceptions to the general rule, and there are some instances where it is used in an active sense.[11] Herein is the dilemma of interpreters.

If it is understood to be active, it means that the church is the "complement" which makes Christ "full," or "complete." As the head is not complete without the body, so Christ is not complete without his mystical body, the church. Much is to be said for this "active" sense. Christ has completed his all-sufficient work of redemption at Calvary. When he shouted with a loud voice from the cross, "It is finished," his work was indeed complete. Yet he left work for his disciples to accomplish too, promising them hardship and persecution; and now it is up to the church to complement the work of Christ with its own work. He depends on us to do our part, as he did his. The all-sufficient efficacy of Calvary now awaits the faithfulness of the church. In this sense, the church may be said to be the "complement" (*pleroma*) of Christ.

If, on the other hand, "fullness" (*pleroma*) is understood as passive, the meaning is that the church, as Christ's body, is filled with his presence, his power, and his graces, and is therefore fully equipped for its mission. Whereas Christ's presence may be thought of as universal, "filling all in all," the church is especially the recipient of his presence and all of the blessings attendant thereto.

To be said in favor of this interpretation is the fact that elsewhere Paul speaks of individual Christians as being filled with the fullness of Christ. In Colossians, just after he has said that in Christ the whole fullness of deity dwells bodily, he continues, "And you have come to fullness of life in him" (2:10). Paul could say this out of his own experience of mystical union with Christ.

In Ephesians, Paul prays for his friends that they might "be filled with all the fullness of God" (3:19). It is but a single step to speak of the corporate people of God, the church, as being filled with the indwelling Spirit of God, or, as in Ephesians 1:23, filled with the fullness of Christ (cf. Jn 1:14–16).

Whether in Ephesians 1:23 we interpret "fullness" (*pleroma*) as active or passive, each interpretation has a valid and meaningful truth. The fact that scholars are about equally divided in their interpretation at this point would indicate that something is to be said on each side. While scholars argue the fine points, why may not we accept each side as having a valid truth and so profit from both? The church, as the "continuing incarnation," the mystical body of Christ, is the very instrument of God for taking the perfect and all-sufficient work of Christ at Calvary and conveying it to an otherwise lost world, thus adding to and complementing the work of Christ for the redemption of mankind. But the church does not, and indeed cannot, act alone. In the process it is *filled* with the presence, power, and all the graces of Christ himself. This is "the fullness of the church."

The Self-Emptying of the Church

In an earlier chapter (Chapter 3), we saw how Christ identified himself with the messianic role of God's "servant." Thus he has left us an example, "that we should follow in his steps" (1 Pet 2:21).

By both example and precept, Jesus sought to instill into his disciples the principles of servanthood. These principles call essentially for humility, self-giving, and a caring love which puts others above self. How diligently and repeatedly he tried to teach these lessons to his disciples.

On one occasion, after the twelve had been arguing among themselves as to which of them was the greatest, he said to them, "If any one would be first, he must be last of all and servant of all" (Mk 9:35). He then took a child in his arms and said, "Whoever receives this child in my name receives me, and whoever receives me receives him who sent me; for he who is least among you all is the one who is great" (Lk 9:48; cf. Mk 9:37).

This dramatic lesson had only limited effect, for shortly thereafter James and John were asking for chief seats in the coming kingdom. When the other apostles learned of it, they were indignant. Jesus called them all together and said:

> You know that those who are supposed to rule over the Gentiles lord it over them, and their great men exercise authority over them. But it shall not be so among you; but whoever would be great among you must be your servant, and whoever would be first among you must be slave of all. For the Son of Man also came not to be served but to serve, and to give his life a ransom for many (Mk 10:42–45).

In the upper room, he gave them one of their most memorable lessons. At some point in the evening's proceedings, he rose from the table, laid aside his garments, and girded himself with a towel. He then poured water into a basin and began to wash the disciples' feet and to wipe them with the towel. Peter protested, but his protest was turned back by Jesus' insistence. The task having been completed, he resumed his place and said:

Do you know what I have done to you? You call me Teacher and Lord; and you are right, for so I am. If I, then, your Lord and teacher, have washed your feet, you also ought to wash one another's feet. For I have given you an example, that you should do as I have done to you. Truly, truly I say to you, a servant is not greater than his master; nor is he who is sent greater than he who sent him. If you know these things, blessed are you if you do them (Jn 13:12–17).

The servant Lord calls for a servant church! We know these things; the question is: Are we doing them? It is fairly easy to look at the church in retrospect and see that there have been times in church history when the church has grossly deviated from the course of servanthood. As Christianity became the state religion under Constantine and the church took on prestige and power, it became easier to define Christ's Lordship in terms of Caesar than of servant. In the middle ages when the church exercised both ecclesiastical and political authority, many of the church's prelates looked upon themselves as lords to be served rather than servants of the people.

Today, we would all profess verbally that the church exists to be servant to people in the name of Christ. In actuality, however, when we are really candid and honest with ourselves, we must confess that the church finds it easier to be Christ's patron than his servant. We acknowledge his Lordship in our creeds, in our hymns, and in our preaching, but we do not want him to be too demanding or specific in his instructions. We want the right to interpret. We reserve the right to choose when, where, and whom we will serve. We are still in control!

While the church has emphasized Christ as savior, it has not taken as seriously his model as servant, preferring to map out its own strategies, with prime consideration being given to local facilities, programs, and budgets to serve its own needs. Too much of its concern is introverted. Most of the local church's efforts and finances go to maintain the local institution. Enough is given to benevolences, including mission causes abroad, to soothe its conscience and make it appear respectable. Its "sacrificial offerings" are usually a misnomer in the light of the world's needs and the affluence of its members.

Someone has well said, "God does not need our sacrifices but he has, nevertheless, appointed a representative to receive them, namely, our neighbor. The neighbor always represents the invisible Christ."[12] Let us not quibble over the question, "And who is my neighbor?" In many ways the church, sent into the world to serve, has adopted the world's standards, measuring success in terms of fine buildings, number of members, and size of the budget.

Happily, there are exceptions to what has just been said. There are some churches that are earnestly and sincerely seeking to serve the needs of their communities, as well as broader concerns, and are truly committed to servanthood. These churches keep faith and hope alive within the total ecumenical church as they remind us of our reason for being.

The members of the clergy are not entirely without blame, for they are the leaders of the churches, and in most cases the churches echo the thinking of the clergy. Members of the clergy need to examine and reexamine themselves on the question of servanthood. It is easy to lose sight of the idealism of the original "call" and to adopt the standards of the world in seeking the larger parish or executive position that offers the higher salary and perquisites rather than the place of lowly service where the real needs exist.

When Jesus sent out the twelve, he charged them "to take nothing for their journey except a staff; no bread, no bag, no money in their belts; but to wear sandals and not put on two tunics" (Mk 6:8–10). They were to travel light. These instructions cannot be lived literally today, but there is a principle here too easily overlooked or evaded. In a day when churches are expected to provide adequate salaries and allowances, it is easy for the minister to succumb to the temptation "What's in it for me?" which is quite the opposite theme from servanthood.

It is not that members of the clergy should be expected to be married to Franciscan poverty, or that we should attempt to turn the clock back to the days when the minister was expected to supplement his meager salary by farming on the side, or when the members of a congregation "pounded" their pastor and his family once or twice a year with canned goods and other staples to tide them over. Scripture reminds us: "The laborer deserves his wages" (1 Tim 5:18). There is a happy medium someplace, which is difficult to find. But we are not released from the obligation of seeking it. Above all, we are to be faithful stewards of whatever comes into our hands.

Whether members of the cloth or members of the congregation, we must ever keep before ourselves the fact that we are a "servant church" serving a "servant Lord."

The church today lays great stress on the observance of the eucharist, as it should. The real presence of Christ, we say, comes to us as in faith we receive the bread and the cup. But can we forget the basin and the towel of the upper room? Not that the basin and the towel should be made into a sacrament, as some churches have done. In a day when people wore sandals and walked dusty roads, the washing of feet had a special significance that would be difficult to recapture in our day of automobiles and mass transit. The symbolic meaning, however, is as valid today as when Jesus performed the act. The real presence of Christ is found also as we make use of the basin and the towel, however their symbolism is translated for us today; for these are the marks of him "who came not to be served but to serve." In rendering a service "to one of the least of these," we do it to him. "If you know these things, blessed are you if you do them" (Jn 13:17).

Fulfillment Through Servanthood

If on the one hand the church is in grave peril of failing to meet the standards of servanthood, on the other hand it is challenged with the glorious possibility of truly being Christ's servant in the world.

Both the spiritual and physical needs in the world today are perhaps of the greatest magnitude of any period in recorded history. The physical and material needs persist despite the high degree of knowledge and technology existing side by side. We have a high degree of knowledge and expertise in agriculture to the point of curtailing crops, while people in some nations are starving or are grossly malnourished. By the medium of television, the physical needs of various people of the world are flashed before us. It is not so easy to visualize their spiritual and mental needs, but these must be of equal or even greater magnitude. In any case, a ministry is needed to the whole person.

The church today is called to act, to be God's servant to all who suffer for whatever reasons. Governments in some cases can assist, if they will, but, as has been demonstrated time and again, such assistance often becomes bogged down in red tape, or is siphoned off at top levels, and help never arrives for the truly needy at the bottom rung of the social ladder. The church is called to respond to the limits of its physical, material, and spiritual resources. To those who say that the church should confine itself to the gospel, I would agree, provided they take seriously Matthew 25 (the final judgment scene), Luke 10 (the good Samaritan), and Luke 16 (the parable of the rich man and Lazarus), to mention only a few passages. A gospel of faith without works is dead! We do Jesus a disservice if we try to separate a gospel of salvation from a gospel that seeks to feed the hungry and clothe the naked.

The Macedonian call, "Come over and help us," came not only to Paul. The needs in many countries cry out for our help. At the same time, this does not mean that we are to be sensitive to needs halfway around the world while neglecting those at our own doorstep. It is not a case of either-or, but both.

The church's integrity is at stake here, but, more, its very life. Jesus said to his disciples, "Whoever would save his life will lose it; but whoever loses his life for my sake will find it" (Mt 16:25). This paradoxical statement presents us with a universal principle of life. To become self-centered is to lose one's life in the worst sort of way. The introverted person loses interest in life and becomes a bore to others. The way to find one's life is to give it away in loving, caring service for others.

Recall the life of Albert Schweitzer as a well-known and notable example. A highly educated man, he held doctorates in three fields: theology, philosophy and music. He was an authority on the life and music of Bach and was himself one of Europe's greatest organists. He was likewise an authority on the life and writings of Goethe. He became well-known in theological circles, especially for his scholarly and timely book, *The Quest of the Historical Jesus.* In spite of his intellectual achievements, he had within himself a burning desire to serve the lowliest of the low and the neediest of the needy. Especially was he burdened with the thought of the great suffering that the white man had brought to Africa through the slave trade. He wanted to repay that debt insofar as humanly possible. He took upon himself the white man's burden.

Resigning his professorship at the University of Strasbourg, he spent seven years at medical school. Meanwhile his wife took training to become a nurse. Then, at the age of thirty-eight, with limited means and staff, he went to Lambarene in French Equatorial Africa to establish a hospital. From one small building, the hospital grew and the work increased as people of many countries, inspired by his sacrificial example, responded to assist.

It did not take long for him to become the trusted friend of the natives. As the news spread, some people walked hundreds of miles, some of them carrying their sick, to receive the miraculous cures wrought at the hands of the white man. For fifty-two years he labored as a servant to the black man. The $33,000 which he was awarded as the recipient of the Nobel Peace Prize in 1952 was donated for further improvements at the hospital and to establish a colony for lepers. His life became a legend, the subject of numerous articles and a number of books, and the inspiration of millions. Someone has said that his greatest contribution was not in what he did himself, but in what others have done because of him. His life furnishes a shining example of one who found his life by losing it.

The principle of finding one's self by losing it applies to the corporate church as well as to individuals. The church, being made up of individual members, may be said to get its texture from them; but the reverse is also true, that the individual members receive inspiration, strength, and motivation from the corporate people of God. Even though members of a particular church may be the scattered church most of the time, as they seek to be Christ's servants in the world they have a sense of being upheld by the thoughts, prayers, and love of their fellow Christians. Even when they are the scattered church, they not only represent the church; they *are* the church, wherever they happen to be, and have Christ's presence with them according to his promise. This realization is a source of great peace and joy.

Trying to be Christ's "servant church" in contemporary settings carries no guarantee that we shall be free from frustrations and hardships. No such promises were given by Jesus to his disciples. Those who sincerely try to walk in Jesus' steps, as they believe he would walk in today's world, must be prepared for possible ridicule and misrepresentation. They must be prepared for rejection by some of their business associates whose lives may move in different orbits. There have been many instances of loss of jobs when personal integrity has conflicted with unethical corporate business practices.

The apostle Paul could tell us much about misrepresentation and suffering loss. There were times when he stood up to his opponents with all the force of his being. There were other times when he found it wise to bow out of the picture and move on. But in all of his conflicts and sufferings, he allowed nothing to come between him and his sense of the divine presence with him guiding and sustaining him, and nothing to dim his high vision of the church as the very instrument of God's redemptive purpose. Any hardships and deprivations were as nothing in comparison to the grace which he received as an apostle and servant of Jesus Christ.

Even so, whatever sacrifices and hardships as we may incur are outweighed many times over by the grace which we receive in Jesus Christ. The sacrifices and hardships, if and when they come, are to be considered a privilege (Phil 1:29). In so serving, sacrificing, and giving of itself, the church finds its true identity and its fulfillment.

Thus the church is filled with the plenitude of God's grace and equipped to serve, and as it serves others its own life is fulfilled and continually renewed in the Spirit. In the light of this the church must never permit itself to become discouraged, disheartened, or dismayed, no matter how difficult the circumstances. It is God's creation, commissioned by Christ himself and empowered by the Holy Spirit, to fulfill God's eternal purpose in the world. There is no task too small, nor any person too low, to be the focus of our ministry. Nor shall any deed of compassion lose its reward. There is no badge of honor that exceeds that of being a disciple of Jesus Christ, and there is no membership in any other institution that compares with being a member of the body of Christ, the church.

It is fitting that we bring this chapter on the church and this book to a close with a doxology from the pen of Paul:

> Now to him who is able to do superabundantly more than we ask or think, according to the power at work in us, to him be the glory in the church and in Christ Jesus unto all generations for ever and ever. Amen.[13]

Notes

Introduction

1. Robert Browning, *A Death in the Desert.*

2. Pleroma—The "Fullness of God" in Jesus Christ

1. With the passing of time, in the Gnostic systems of the second and third centuries, *pleroma* was sometimes used to refer to God, and sometimes to *the place* where God dwelt in highest heaven. I take it that this was a later development, beyond Paul's time, and need not concern us here. The Gnostics were not consistent in their use of terms. Consistency was not one of their virtues! This, I suppose, was by design to add to the complexity and mystery of their teachings.

2. E.F. Scott, *The Moffatt New Testament Commentary, The Epistles of Paul to the Colossians, to Philemon, and to the Ephesians,* pp. 41, 51, 54.

3. There are many scripture passages to substantiate Jesus' teaching of his unique relationship to God. A few are: Mt 11:2–6, 27–30; 12:6–8, 42; Mk 2:5–12; 14:61–62; Lk 20:9–16. The entire gospel of John would stand as an affirmation of Jesus' unique Sonship and his knowledge of the same.

4. The servant passages in Isaiah are: 41:8–10; 42:1–9, 18–20; 44:1–2, 21–23; 49:1–13; 50:4–9; 52:13–53:12; 61:1–4. For references to the servant role in the gospels, see Mt 10:25; 20:26–28; Mk 10:42–45; Lk 4:18–21; 12:37; 22:27.

5. Some of the passages in the Old Testament looking toward a kingly messiah are: Is 2:1–4, 9:6–7; 11:1–9; Jer 23:5–6; 33:14–16; Ez 34:23; 37:24; Zech 9:9–10; Pss 2; 89; 110; 132:11–18. There are other passages. Echoes of the expectation of a kingly messiah are seen in Mark 10:35–37 and Acts 1:6.

6. Some of the passages in which Wisdom is personified are:

131

Prv 1:20–33; 8:1–9:6; Job 28:12–27. From the Apocrypha, Sir 24; Wis 6:12–10:21. There are other passages.

7. C.H. Dodd, *A Companion to the Bible,* ed. T.W. Manson, p. 409.

8. J.B. Lightfoot, *Saint Paul's Epistles to the Colossians and to Philemon,* p. 261.

9. For other examples of God's presence filling heaven and earth, see: 1 Kgs 8:27; Jer 23:24; Is 6:1; 66:1. From the Apocrypha, Wis 1:6–7; 8:1. There are numerous other examples.

10. Paul's quotation, "In him we live and move and have our being," is attributed to Epimenides, a poet and naturalist of Crete of the sixth century B.C.

11. For examples from Philo of God's filling all things by means of his Spirit, or Logos, or Wisdom, or Providence, or his powers, see: *Legum Allegoria,* III, ii, 4; *De Gigantibus,* VI, 27–28; *De Specialibus Legibus,* I, iii, 18; *De Vita Mosis,* II, xliii, 238; and many other places.

12. For other examples from Philo of God's filling all things but not being contained, see: *De Migratione Abrahami,* XXXII, 181–182; XXXV, 192; *De Confusione Linguarum,* XXVII, 136; *Legum Allegoria,* I, xiv, 44.

13. For a good discussion of Christ's victory over the world powers, see Alan Richardson, *An Introduction to the Theology of the New Testament,* pp. 211ff.

3. Kenosis—The "Self-Emptying" of Jesus Christ

1. Ernest Lohmeyer, *Kyrios Jesus,* pp. 5ff. See also his Commentary, *Die Briefe an die Philipper, an die Kolosser und an Philemon.*

2. References to "servant" (*doulos*) and "servant" (*pais*) in Deutero-Isaiah: *Doulos:* Is 42:19; 48:20; 49:3, 5; 53:11; 63:17. *Pais:* Is 41:8; 42:1; 44:1, 2, 21; 45:4; 49:6; 50:10; 52:13.

3. See note 5 of Chapter 2.

4. The term Son of Man is also used by Ezekiel of himself as God's lowly servant. It is used repeatedly in the pseudepigraphic writing known as Ethiopic Enoch or 1 Enoch, especially chapters 37–71 known as the Similitudes. 1 Enoch is a composite work with different sources. Chapters 37–71 are dated around 100–80 B.C. This work may, or may not, have entered into Jesus' use of

the term. For our purpose we see no need to go beyond the references in Daniel and Ezekiel.

5. For examples of how Jewish interpreters twisted the natural meaning of Isaiah 52–53, see William Manson, *Jesus the Messiah,* pp. 168–170.

6. For examples of Old Testament passages which referred originally to the God of Israel, now used of Christ, see Acts 4:26; 1 Cor 1:31; 10:9, 22; 15:25.

7. Other examples where one cannot tell whether the author is referring to God the Father or Jesus Christ as Lord: Acts 1:24; 7:60; 9:10, 31; 10:14; 11:21; 12:11; and other places.

8. For a history of *kenoticism* from the time of the church fathers until 1881 (the date of publication), the finest work, to my knowledge, is still A.B. Bruce, *The Humiliation of Christ.* Special mention should also be made of Oscar Bensow, *Die Lehre von der Kenose;* Herbert M. Relton, *A Study in Christology;* and Friedrich Loof's article, "Kenosis," in *Hastings' Encyclopedia of Religion and Ethics.* An excellent more modern work is by Donald G. Dawe, *The Form of a Servant.* Some of the other writers and their works are: Wolfgang F. Gess, *Die Lehre von der Person Christi;* and *Christi Person und Werk;* Gottfried Thomasius, *Christi Person und Werk,* Vol. II; A.M. Fairbairn, *The Person of Christ in Modern Theology;* Charles Gore, *Dissertations on Subjects Connected With the Incarnation; The Incarnation of the Son of God;* and *Belief in Christ;* Frank Weston, *The One Christ;* William Temple, *Christus Veritas,* chapter VIII; P.T. Forsyth, *The Person and Place of Jesus Christ;* H.R. Mackintosh, *The Person of Jesus Christ,* especially Chapter I on "The Self-Limitation of God in Christ."

9. References to the phrase "whom God raised up": Acts 2:24, 32; 3:15, 26; 4:10; 5:30; 10:40; and elsewhere.

10. Donald Baillie, *God Was in Christ,* p. 132.

4. The Relevance of the Paradox to the Incarnation

1. Reinhold Niebuhr, *Beyond Tragedy,* pp. 13, 16.

2. Wolfhart Pannenberg, *Jesus—God and Man,* p. 34.

3. *Ibid.,* pp. 33–37, 53ff, 67f, 134ff, 301, 307, and elsewhere.

4. Victor Weisskoff, quoted from my memory of his statement in a TV documentary.

5. For insights on *plerosis* through *kenosis,* I am much indebted to P.T. Forsyth's chapter, "The *Plerosis* or the Self-Fulfillment of

Christ," in his book, *The Person and Place of Jesus Christ,* pp. 321ff.

6. William Temple, *Christus Veritas,* p. 144. The same thought is given in his book, *Readings in St. John's Gospel,* p. 14.

7. Other scripture references suggesting Christ's glorification following his humiliation: Lk 24:26; Heb 2:9; 12:2; 1 Pet 1:11.

5. The Relevance of the Paradox
to the Atonement

1. From William Wordsworth's poem "Intimations of Immortality."

2. Melanchthon's statement, quoted by Wolfhart Pannenberg, *Jesus—God and Man,* p. 38.

3. Wolfhart Pannenberg, *Jesus—God and Man,* p. 38.

4. Raymond Abba in an article on "Propitiation" in *The Interpreter's Dictionary of the Bible,* Volume 3, pp. 920f. Other references to the same effect: C.H. Dodd, *The Bible and the Greeks,* pp. 82–95; *The Epistle of Paul to the Romans,* Moffatt New Testament Commentary, pp. 54–55; G.B. Gray, *Sacrifice in the Old Testament,* pp. 55–95; Vincent Taylor, *Jesus and His Sacrifice,* pp. 50–53.

5. Scripture references regarding the sin sacrifice and guilt sacrifice include the following chapters: Lev 4–6; 12; 14; 16; Num 5; 6; 15; 28; 29.

6. Other prophetic denunciations of the sacrificial system are: Am 5:21–24; Hos 6:6; Mi 6:6–8; Jer 6:20; 7:21–23.

7. Plato, *The Republic,* Book II, 361 E.

8. William Manson, *Jesus, The Messiah,* pp. 131–34.

9. William Manson, *The Gospel of Luke,* Moffatt New Testament Commentary, p. 241.

10. Some of the New Testament passages connecting the passion of Jesus to Isaiah 53: Mt 8:17; Lk 24:25–27; Jn 1:29; Acts 3:13, 18; 4:27; 8:32–35; 1 Pet 2:21–25; Heb 9:28.

11. For translation "sufferings," see *The Jerusalem Bible,* with footnote; also *The Interpreter's Bible,* Vol. 5, p. 630.

12. An example of the idea of expiation being made by individuals for the nation is found in late Judaism in IV Maccabees (c. first half of first century A.D.) where it is said that the blood of the martyrs who perished during the Maccabean revolt has overcome the power of tyranny, cleansed the fatherland, and renewed the observance of the law (1:11; 17:21; 18:4). "They have become as

it were a substitute for the sin of the nation, and through the blood of these pious ones and their expiatory death the divine providence has preserved Israel" (17:21–22; cf. 6:27–29).

13. Donald Baillie, *God Was in Christ*, pp. 173f. I have taken the liberty of changing his wording somewhat.

14. *Ibid.*, p. 173.

15. For other Pauline references regarding redemption, see Rom 3:24; 1 Cor 1:30; Gal 3:13; 5:1; Col 1:14; and other places.

16. Other Pauline references to justification and righteousness are: Rom 1:17; 3:20–4:25; 5:1–21; 6:15–19; 8:30–34; 10:1–13; 1 Cor 1:30; 6:11; 2 Cor 5:21; Gal 2:15–21; Phil 3:6–9. On this subject, helpful references (among many) are: C.H. Dodd, *The Epistle of Paul to the Romans, Moffatt New Testament Commentary*, pp. 8–13; 51–53; Vincent Taylor's chapter on "Justification" in his book, *Forgiveness and Reconciliation*, pp. 29–69; Alan Richardson, *An Introduction to the Theology of the New Testament*, pp. 232–40.

17. A helpful reference is Vincent Taylor's chapter on "Reconciliation" in his book, *Forgiveness and Reconciliation*, pp. 70–108.

18. C.H. Dodd, *The Epistle of Paul to the Romans, The Moffatt New Testament Commentary*, p. 54. His more complete dissertation on the subject is found in his book, *The Bible and the Greeks*, pp. 82–95; also in *Journal of Theological Studies*, Vol. XXXII, pp. 352–360. Other helpful references: Vincent Taylor, *Jesus and His Sacrifice*, pp. 50–53; G.B. Gray, *Sacrifice in the Old Testament*, pp. 55–95.

19. Other scripture references to eternal life as the result of Christ's saving work are: Rom 2:10; 5:20–21; 6:5–8; 8:1–39; 1 Cor 15:12–57; 2 Cor 5:1, 17; Col 1:27; 3:4; and others.

20. The historic nature of the atonement is portrayed in many places. Examples: Rom 3:25; 5:6–11; Col 1:19–20, 22. Cf. Heb 2:11–18; 4:15; 5:7–10; and other places.

21. The Adam comparisons: Rom 5:12–21; 6:23; 1 Cor 15:20–27, 45–50.

6. The Relevance of the Paradox to the Church

1. For other passages depicting Israel as God's own possession, treasure, people, see Dt 4:20; 7:6; 14:2; 26:18. Compare KJV, "a peculiar people."

2. My translation. The Revised Standard Version does not cap-

ture the real impact of the Greek, that Christians are God's own treasure, as Israel was in the Old Testament (Dt 32:9).

3. For other passages depicting Israel as the spouse of God, see Is 50:1; 54:6–8; Jer 2:2; and other places.

4. God, spoken of as a jealous God: Ex 20:5; 34:14; Dt 4:24; 5:9; Jos 24:19; and other places.

5. Israel's infidelity as God's spouse: Ex 34:15–16; Lev 20:5–6; Hos 2:5; 4:13–15; 9:1; Is 1:21; Jer 2:20; 3:1, 6, 8; Ez 16:15ff; 21:1ff; and other places.

6. References of Jesus to the bridegroom: Mt 22:1–10; 25:1–13; Lk 12:35–40.

7. Passages suggesting the cleansing effect of God's word: Pss 19:8–9; 119:9, 11, 130, 160; Jn 15:3; 17:17; Heb 4:12; 1 Pet 1:22–23.

8. Among the theories of the origin of the concept of the church as the body of Christ, comparisons are made to the rabbinic teaching of the oneness of mankind in Adam, and to the Greeks' analogy of the body to the commonwealth: Plato, *Republic*, V. 462. See Alan Richardson, *An Introduction to the Theology of the New Testament*, p. 255.

9. On the point that the church is in reality the mystical body of Christ (not just a figure of speech), see Clarence T. Craig, *The Interpreter's Bible*, Vol. 10, p. 156. Also, reference is made to L.S. Thornton, *The Common Life in the Body of Christ*, where the idea is worked out in great detail.

10. Quoted from memory from the late Dr. W.R. Wilson, Professor of Homiletics, Pittsburgh-Xenia Theological Seminary.

11. The term *pleroma* is used in an active sense in scripture to refer to the patch on an old garment, thus making the garment complete (Mt 9:16; Mk 2:21). In secular Greek it is used of a ship's crew in the sense of "complement" to the ship, the ship being incomplete without its crew: Xenophon, *Hellenica*, V, i, 11; VI, ii, 35; Philo, *Quod Omnis Probus Liber Sit*, XX, 142; Thucydides, *History of the Peloponnesian War*, VII, iv, 6; VII, xiv, 1. It is also used in an active sense to designate the different segments or "complements," of society: Aristotle, *Politics*, IV, iii, 12 (1291a, 17); III, viii, 1 (1284a, 5). For one commentator who contends for the active sense of *pleroma* in Ephesians 1:23, see J. Armitage Robinson's commentary, *St. Paul's Epistle to the Ephesians*, ad loc., and a detached note on *Pleroma*, pp. 255ff.

12. J.S. Whale, *Christian Doctrine*, p. 145.

13. Eph 3:20–21 (author's translation).

Index of Subjects and Persons

Index of Scripture References